114527

S0-CBQ-995

Always Being Reformed

By John C. Purdy

Parables at Work

Edited by John C. Purdy

Always Being Reformed: The Future of Church Education

Always Being Reformed
The Future of Church Education

Edited by John C. Purdy

The Geneva Press
Philadelphia

Copyright © 1985 The Geneva Press

All rights reserved—no part of this book may be reproduced in any form without permission in writing from the publisher, except by a reviewer who wishes to quote brief passages in connection with a review in magazine or newspaper.

The quotation on page 88 from *Time*, October 15, 1984, is copyright 1984 Time Inc. All rights reserved. Reprinted by permission from TIME.

Book design by Gene Harris

First edition

Published by The Geneva Press℞
Philadelphia, Pennsylvania

PRINTED IN THE UNITED STATES OF AMERICA

9 8 7 6 5 4 3 2 1

Library of Congress Cataloging in Publication Data

Main entry under title:

Always being reformed

    1. Christian education—Addresses, essays,
lectures. 2. Reformed Church—Education—Addresses,
essays, lectures. I. Purdy, John C. (John Clifford),
1925–
BV1473.A45 1985   207   85–953
ISBN 0–664–24655–9 (pbk.)

07
193

L. I. F. E. Bible College
LIBRARY
1100 COVINA BLVD
SAN DIMAS, CA 91773

Contents

039683

Contributors   119

Preface

Most of the current beneficiaries of church education will live most of their days in the next century. Think about that. When we educators think about it, we get uneasy—on two counts. First, none of us knows what the twenty-first century will be like; we know only that when it arrives it will be other than what we now imagine. Fifteen years ago, who of us could have imagined Music TV, cheap home computers, gas at $1.16 a gallon, and a media star in the White House? How can we hold tight to education as preparation today for life tomorrow? If tomorrow never comes, of what good is such training?

So our minds turn to other notions of education, such as nourishing the roots so that the plant can flower and bear fruit. But where are our roots? What is the essence of the Presbyterian (Reformed) tradition? We are not sure; that is the second cause of our unease. We have been so busy equipping our children and youth for life in today's world that we have at best a tenuous grasp on what is of permanent value out of our past.

Uneasy about both our future and our past, 134 Presbyterian educators met in April of 1984 at Montreat, North Carolina, to consider our ministry. We were greatly enlivened by a lecture on "Always to Be Reformed" by

Edward A. Dowey. (It prompted this collection of essays; most of the contributors were in the audience.) In Dowey's assessment was balm for our uneasiness. Hearing ourselves described as "the church reformed" assured us that there is much of value in our tradition; hearing that the church is "always to be reformed" gave us liberty to reshape and reform our tradition to meet the challenges of the present.

As you read the essays in this book, listen for two notes. Listen for an openness to change, to voices calling for the church "to be reformed." Listen also for a loving appreciation of the God who has brought us to this moment and for a corresponding acceptance of the path by which we have been brought. If we educators reconstruct, reshape, reform our ministry in such a way as to be faithful both to our present and to our past, we can face the twenty-first century with a good conscience—in whatever form it greets us.

JOHN C. PURDY

1

Always
to Be Reformed

Edward A. Dowey

Reform is always a benign term in church history, as it is in politics. It is not used in a bad sense. It is never willingly applied to changes or developments that one regards as decline, falling away, or disaster. Reform always means improvement. Indeed, when Reformed became a proper name favored for what was otherwise called Calvinism, there was a reluctance to use it, especially in Catholic countries. In seventeenth-century France when Protestants indicated religious affiliation on legal papers, they were required to write "so-called [*prétendu*] Reformed." This would cast no aspersions on possibly unreformed or deformed religion!

There is a popular old slogan that has been very prominent in the European Reformed tradition, although almost unknown on the American scene until recent years. It is almost always used in Latin: *Ecclesia reformata, semper reformanda*. This translates as "The church reformed and always to be reformed." It appeared on the provisional seal of the uniting General Assembly when the Presbyterian Church (U.S.A.) was formed. It appears, wrongly translated, in the Presbyterian Form of Government, chapter II, as "always reforming." The verb is passive. The church is the object, not the subject of reform. The completion of the slogan, universally understood, is found in words often printed as a part of it: namely, "according to the Word of God" (*secundum verbum Dei*). A full paraphrase of the meaning might be: The church long ago reformed according to the Word of God must always be reformed according to the Word of God.

All would agree that the people of God throughout the Bible are called into being by the divine Word and are recalled to their true vocation in the same way. If so, the prophets and apostles were reformers, and the oldest Christian reforming literature is found in the epistles of Paul. Paul called on the churches of Corinth, Colossae, and Galatia to be true to the gospel as they first heard it and from which they had fallen away. Unlike such terms as revolt or revolution, where the attempt is made to destroy the past and begin something new, the motif here is the recovery of something old.

But not merely old: Reform according to the Word of God is not antiquarian or simplistic; the Protestant Reformers did not expect people to turn back the calendar and become again simple Galilean fishermen. It was the recovery in their own day of the word "contained in" the Scriptures (French Confession, 1559) that they preached and applied to both the most cultured and the simplest of their contemporaries.

Reform has a backward and a forward reference. It leads not only back to the Bible but also forward under the word. The Second Helvetic Confession (1566) teaches that "from these Scriptures are to be derived true wisdom and godliness, the reformation and government of churches," and also, "when this Word of God is now preached in the church . . . the very Word of God is proclaimed, and received by the faithful." The Presbyterian Confession of 1967 carries this forward by teaching, "As God has spoken [God's] word in diverse cultural situations, the church is confident that [God] will continue to speak through the

Scriptures in a changing world and in every form of human culture."

Reform that listens to the past and looks to the future must be guarded against two dangers. One is biblicism, which tries to find literal and specific direction for everything in the words of the Bible, as if there were no gap in time between the Bible and ourselves. This way of procedure tends to belittle necessary interpretation (the hermeneutic process) and often ingeniously distorts the Bible into our present situation or skews the present toward some archaic condition from Bible times. Such literalism has held that if Paul sent a slave back to his master—or rejected women as officeholders in the church—so should we! The other, opposite danger is so to adjust and update the Bible to the modern scene that it can say only what we already know. Scripture is thus reduced to supplying illustrations of ideas or actions derived from current fashions of thought or action. The modern scene and current practices become a kind of censor over what the Bible is allowed to say. By this process the word loses its message and the church ceases to be the church.

When the word is overlaid by church traditions and habitual responses, or when it is endangered by outside forces, political or social or scientific, it is muffled, unclear, or even silent. Only when the word breaks through again, as in Luther, the classic Reformer, is the church called back and called forward to its true destiny.

Reform is very close to repentance and rebirth. One might say it is the ecclesial or communal dimension of repentance. Renewal or reform of the church is not merely the aggregate of individual renewals, it is an essential element of all renewal, sharing the polarity of all human life between the personal and the societal.

Like repentance and rebirth, reform can be seen in one sense as a continuing process. But it also appears as an episodic process, in that special times and qualities of re-

form deserve the name more clearly than others. Witness
the many reformations so designated in church history. In
an American society that is obsessed with change and progress, often to the point of mindless tinkering and scorn of
history, we might be too ready to label our best efforts
reformatory. They must be. But it might be wiser to let
history designate reforms after the fact, at the same time
that we remain open to and obedient to the prompting of
word and Spirit in the church "always to be reformed."

Confessions as Biblical Interpretation

By the Word of God we do not mean the Bible as such;
we mean the revelation or self-disclosure of God as gracious love in Jesus Christ, of which the Bible is the witness
and instrument. Confessing Christ and confessional statements belong not to revelation but to the human response
to revelation in the church. The response is always an
interpretation made up in part from those who do the
confessing. The whole life of the church is a response to
and an interpretation of biblical revelation. This is the
point of Gerhard Ebeling's brilliant essay, "Church History as the History of the Interpretation of Holy Scripture"
(*The Word of God and Tradition*; Fortress, 1968).

By interpretation Ebeling does not mean merely exe-
gesis, or teaching, or preaching and doctrine, but everything in church life. He includes ritual and prayer, theological work and personal decisions, church organization
and ecclesiastical politics, the temporal power of the pa-
pacy, the ecclesiastical pretensions of rulers, wars of religion and works of compassionate love, the promotion of
Christian culture and cloistered renunciation of the world,
martyrdoms and witch burnings. "By the term 'interpretation,' " writes Ebeling, "we are to understand a relation
to Holy Scripture which is not only spoken but unspoken,

not only conscious but also unconscious, not only positive but negative."

It is clusters of these responses with their various configurations that make up the various traditions and families of traditions in world Christianity. One of these, the Reformed, is a tradition especially of the word, elevating preaching, teaching (doctrine), and ethical practice to the forefront of its concerns. Thus confessional documents have always had a prominent place in its history, especially in the education and ordination of ministers, and also in catechetical instruction. (Since the demise of the strict catechetical method, confessions have played a mixed and variable role among church educators—sometimes, no role at all.)

Confessions both lead to Scripture and lead from Scripture. They represent a normative consensus of the church about the meaning of Scripture. The Protestant Reformation is a paradigm of this. For Lutherans as well as the Reformed, the doctrine of justification by grace through faith alone became the basic form of the Word of God revealed in Scripture. This was not regarded as one theological topic alongside others but a major reorientation affecting the whole body of Christian teaching. This doctrine was the root of the re-formation in teaching, preaching, worship, and ethos. It would of course be foolish to overlook many other developments that were taking place in the sixteenth century in personal and social psychology, economic, political, and cultural change, and ecclesiastical and liturgical practices of all sorts. Without these the Protestant Reformation could not have taken place. Nonetheless, we are maintaining that Bible hermeneutic was at the center. It was a *corrected interpretation of what the Bible means by grace* that chiefly characterized the Protestant Reformation over against the Radical Baptist, on the one hand, and the reformed Roman Church that issued from the Council of Trent, on the other. The two chief confessional traditions of the Protestant Reformation, Lutheran and Reformed, have always depended heavily for their ongoing life on the guidance and teaching of the interpretation of the Bible found in their confessions.

The epitome of Reformed teaching for the Presbyterian Church (U.S.A.) is found in its *Book of Confessions*. Here are responses of the church to threats and challenges, to liturgical and educational needs, from the earliest centuries to the present. But this is not merely history. Each of these documents says some things in a form that is unsurpassed and still speaks to us. What they teach is in the bloodstream of the tradition and can be renewed by transfusions when needed. Other things are clearly time-bound and have been superseded, intentionally, in subsequent teaching, such as the Westminster doctrine of Scripture by that of the Confession of 1967. When the *Book of Confessions* is well known by preachers and educators, and the historical setting of each document is appreciated, the book becomes a major resource both for Reformed teaching and for teaching "to be reformed."

Traditionalism

Tradition and traditionalism are very different. In the unforgettable expression of Jaroslav Pelikan, "Tradition is the still living thoughts of the dead, and traditionalism consists of the dead thoughts of the living." Tradition lives and grows not merely by repeating itself, imitating ancestors, and parroting and protecting old phrases but by facing new situations in the spirit of a former time, ready to do a new thing if called on. Many years ago when the Daughters of the American Revolution forbade the great soprano Marian Anderson to sing in Constitution Hall because she was black, Bernard De Voto acidly commented that these daughters of revolution would never apparently become mothers of one. Again, traditionalism against tradition.

Closer to home, the American Presbyterian church has

often seemed to walk a chalk line between tradition and traditionalism, occasionally falling into the latter. In 1838 the "Old School" partisans instituted an oath by which seminary professors had to swear "not to inculcate, teach, or insinuate anything which shall appear to me to contradict or contravene, either directly or impliedly, anything taught in the said [Westminster] Confession of Faith . . . while I remain a professor in this seminary." This demonic rigor is out of harmony with Westminster itself, which held that "the purest churches under heaven are subject both to mixture and error" and "all synods or councils since the apostles' times, whether general or particular, may err, and many have erred." This oath survived until the middle of our century. It is the height of irony that a church in the "always to be reformed" tradition should have placed its theological faculties in this procrustean bed. The reason was found in the defensive effort to exclude all elements of modernity (then called "neology," later "modernism") from the faith of the church. Similarly, an effort to revise the Westminster standards failed in 1893, and subsequently several ministers and professors were forced out of the church for nonconforming views.

But a more open sense of tradition was alive from the founding of the Presbyterian church that kept the subscription of ministers free of the stifling narrowness of the teaching oath. What ministers subscribed to was the "system of doctrine" of the Westminster standards as being that of the Scriptures. This phrase, however, was intentionally left undefined. Also, candidates were allowed to declare "scruples," with presbyteries to decide on the acceptability of ordinands in personal face-to-face encounter. There was an effort to define the "system" more closely by listing five fundamentals (hence, "fundamentalist"). Although a pronouncement supporting the five fundamentals was passed by three General Assemblies, they never got into the Form of Government and were finally repudiated by the church's Special Commission of 1925.

Thus emerged "the broadening church," so well described in Lefferts A. Loetscher's book of that title.

In subsequent years a tradition older than Westminster, from the Reformation itself, began to make itself felt and to deepen the faith of the broadening church. The Presbyterian *Christian Faith and Life* curriculum for church schools in the 1940s and 1950s brought together the best of the American Biblical Theology movement with elements of the European revival of theology of that time, and taught the church a profoundly renewed sense of its own biblical, historical, ecumenical, and ethical inheritance. This curriculum paved the way for the confessional renewal, when the *Book of Confessions* and the Confession of 1967 were adopted by the United Presbyterians.

Preaching and Teaching

In Western Christianity, the Reformed tradition in particular has a reputation for emphasis on the word as the center of its life and practice. Hence preaching and teaching have always been prominent; theology plays a larger role than in some other churches; education and educational institutions have been prominent in its history. What, then, is preaching? And what is teaching?

Preaching is primarily announcement; teaching is the educational strategy through which the announcement is made understandable. Preaching is not identical with the Sunday sermon, nor does teaching require a classroom. Either situation is appropriate for either activity, depending on special conditions. Innumerable other situations are appropriate to both. By "preaching" we mean primarily what is preached. Calling it an announcement or a proclamation indicates that what is preached is not to be derived from the hearers or catechized out of them, as Socrates drew geometry from a slave. Rather, it is always fundamentally the underivable, unexpected, sheerly gracious gift of the message of salvation. When put into words or pictures, or any other medium that will carry it, the message is passed along and the church is built up by it. Teaching has more to do with preparing both the recipient and the "preacher," with elaborating the message, and with tracing out its significance. Where the two activities converge, there is no clear dividing line, but where they diverge, these descriptions are apt. Calvin was able to use the same word, *doctrina*, for both preaching and teaching, allowing the context to make the distinction.

The Confession of 1967 holds that effective preaching and teaching require "disciplined study" of both the Bible and the contemporary world. Disciplined study is an important expression. Casual knowledge, or even the diligently pursued interests of lay people, will not suffice for the church in relation either to the Bible (where would we be without scholar-translators?) or to the worlds of culture, natural science, psychology, politics, and economics. The everyday reader of the Bible, like the man-in-the-street voter, can learn a lot. But a treadmill of superficiality results in both instances if finely trained minds and good leadership are not forthcoming. Unless fresh, firsthand work continues to inform both preaching and teaching, the message of the church will quickly come to have the quaint sound of old phonograph records. The Reformation began in the universities; its greatest leaders were learned teachers; it was a rare bird among the minor Reformers who was not a competent scholar.

How, apart from educated knowledge of the world, can the church know where it is rightly "in" the world and where it must see itself as not "of" the world? The gospel can become a cliché of culture. The church can become just one institution among others, indistinguishable from its milieu, if it does not constantly examine its own actual life in the society in which it exists. The church that is not critically aware of its own life in the world, and the world's penetration of the church, will have crippled and deformed its own mission. If the church is truly oriented toward the

future, animated by hope, and confident of God's providence, it will not and cannot be—what it so often appears
to be—a fortress for the defense of everything old-fash-
ioned. Here the educator has a central role to play, on
every level and in many fields of learning. Here we see
the hermeneutic task writ large, and not to be shirked.

Reformed Education

A recent study paper prepared for a conference of church
educators characterized Reformed education under five
headings. Here we comment on that excellent outline.
Reformed education in the context of a ministering church
was said to be biblically grounded, historically informed,
ecumenically involved, socially engaged, and communally
nurtured. To which we add: mission oriented.

Biblically Grounded

The Bible, said Luther, is the cradle in which Christ
lies, and is authoritative to us because it urges Christ upon
us. Calvin, in the same vein, held that the focus of faith
within the Bible is the "gratuitous benevolence of God in
Christ toward us." Scripture as a whole was more universally and uncritically received in the sixteenth century than
it is today; thus it is all the more remarkable that both
these Reformers made a distinction between the biblical
canon, as such, and the center of that to which it bears
witness: the story of redemption. They drew a distinction
between peripheral and central, between setting and sub-
stance, between the book (which they held was inspired
in every detail) and the message of salvation by God's
grace alone, which was the central content or revelation
of both the Old and the New Testament. In our day, when
we know of tens of thousands of variant readings in the
inherited manuscripts of the New Testament and have, for

instance, vastly increased knowledge of the age and origin of the world and of the human race than was formerly available, it is important to know that the central focus was always on the way of salvation, which is untouched by historical and critical Bible study. "Biblically grounded" thus means grounded in Christ, the Word revealed, and not merely on words inspired, for the latter are instrumental and not the word as such. Thus the Spirit guides us into all truth and frees us from fear of cultural and historical change.

This is the message we hear from the Bern Thesis of 1528: "The Holy Christian Church, whose only head is Jesus Christ, is born of the word of God, abides in the same, and heeds not the voice of a stranger." These words lie directly behind the first thesis of the German Protestant Declaration of Barmen: "Jesus Christ, as he is attested for us in Holy Scripture, is the one Word of God which we have to hear and which we have to trust and obey in life and in death." The first word of the church against Hitler was a Reformation word and a biblical word: Christ alone, *Christus solus*.

Historically Informed

This category is so close to the preceding one as to be almost identical, for the revelation of God in Christ came and comes in history. Here, however, we turn more toward the history of the church after biblical times. We immediately become aware of the varied idiom of historical Christianity in different centuries and different parts of the world. The theological idiom of fourth-century Greek Christianity, so hard for us to understand and appreciate, appears as a language in which the whole fate of the church rested on rejecting a diphthong! Not *homoiousion* but *homoousion*. It is probably not much less difficult for us to understand how the phrase "salvation by grace through faith alone" became the fulcrum on which the leverage of the Protestant Reformation rested when it so fatefully moved the world.

Only by a broad historical understanding can we appreciate the strengths and weaknesses of our own Reformed idiom, which affects our faith and life every day whether we realize it or not. All Christians belong to some tradition or other that has made some particular contribution to the understanding of Christianity. We cannot just broad-mindedly speak language itself; we must speak some particular language. Esperanto is a great idea, but it is too shallow to say anything with a richness of meaning. We are, all of us, Christians of a peculiar sort, with a particular heritage, which we need to appreciate to understand our own grounding in the Bible, as well as our own worship and ethos.

Ecumenically Involved

Before ecumenical involvement comes ecumenical identity. "Reformed" and "ecumenical" are not always antonyms. They are, when the subject is well investigated, more nearly synonyms. It was never the purpose of the Reformers to found a new church or to set a separate tradition beside the catholic church. In their self-understanding they were not founders, they were reformers and purifiers of the single, one, and only catholic church. One of the strongest statements in all Christian literature on the oneness of the church is found in the most authoritative of the Reformed confessions, the Second Helvetic Confession, chapter 17: "And since there is always but one God, and there is one mediator between God and [humanity], Jesus the Messiah, and one Shepherd of the whole flock, one Head of this body, and, to conclude, one Spirit, one salvation, one faith, one Testament or covenant, it necessarily follows that there is only one Church." It is this self-conceived identity with the one church, "scattered through all parts of the world, and extended unto all times," as the Confession adds, that prevents the Reformed tradition from being sectarian and separatist. To be Reformed is to be catholic in essence, and to be pained by the sinful, empirical divisions among which we of the one church live.

Therefore, given this theological and faithful identity, the Reformed are by definition also involved in overcoming divisions and separations, with which the history of Christianity is rife, and in many secondary and partial measures that lead in an ecumenical direction. The methods and strategies of ecumenical involvement are to be determined by many kinds of circumstances, but if these activities begin in realization of catholic identity, they are truly ecumenical. Otherwise, they would have to be cast as missionary activities, a very different matter.

Socially Engaged

Throughout its history the Reformed tradition has had a strong ethical impact on the societies in which it has existed. The root of this, theologically, can be stated most conveniently by reference to what the Reformation called the "third use" of the law. The law—compressed in the Ten Commandments and in Jesus' comments on them in the Sermon on the Mount, as well as his summary of the law and the prophets—all this together has its first use in the conviction of sin. A second use is as the moral base of human society, or the "civic" use. The third use is as a guide to the Christian life. The last was especially strong in Calvin, as opposed to Luther, and is found elaborately worked out into a total personal ethic in the Westminster Larger Catechism. Another example is the Heidelberg Catechism, where Part III, called "Thankfulness," contains an analysis of the Decalogue. That is to say, thanksgiving to God for salvation is given in Christian obedience. This is emphatically nonmeritorious obedience, for no one can earn salvation, but thankful obedience, giving thanks for the gift of salvation. This third use is the base of the famed "Calvinist ethic," about which many volumes have been written, crediting among other things the dominance of capitalism in the West to Calvinist self-motivated hard work, done to the glory of God. Whether such sociological theory is in fact wholly accurate is not our concern here. Certainly, however, aspects of the Reformed ethic can clearly be seen to have earned something of this reputation.

The rubric with which we are working, you will object, is "socially," not "ethically," engaged. There is an important difference. When sin and grace are conceived individualistically, as in the Westminster Catechism, the social is a by-product of individual action. But in our century there has grown a greater awareness of the complete co-inherence of individual life and social life, and of the structural and systemic nature of both sin and grace. Thus, not only the private Christian (really an impossible term) but also the Christian community partake of and accept responsibility for the life of society in which they exist. This is social engagement. The awareness and conviction of this responsibility had been growing for a century before it was formulated confessionally in the Confession of 1967, the section on Reconciliation in Society. "In each time and place there are particular problems and crises through which God calls the church to act. The church, guided by the Spirit, humbled by its own complicity and instructed by all attainable knowledge, seeks to discern the will of God and learn how to obey in these concrete situations." Then follow sample paradigms of social problems: racism, war, poverty, and sexual anarchy.

In this area, education—involving professional research, both theological and societal—and educational strategies are necessary if the church is to fulfill its role. These are often difficult issues with a diversity of view among equally serious Christians, deriving both from social position and from self-interest. All issues must be

treated in mutual forbearance and love, but always oriented by the direction given to Christian consciences in
the law and the teaching of Jesus. Here, especially, the
Reformed tradition is both famous and infamous. In the
European west it uniformly upholds the equality of persons; in South Africa, the Reformed church upholds
apartheid. There is no room for boasting, and much room
for Spirit-guided obedience.

Communally Nurtured

This heading points again—the subject has been near
the surface throughout this series of topics—to the personal and societal polarities and correlations of the Christian community and its members. Strictly speaking there
is no such thing as a private or individual Christian. Faith
always lives in the *koinonia* of the faithful. Even in physical
isolation from other human beings on an uninhabited des-
ert island, the reader of Scripture encounters not solilo-
quies but stories of the people of God, Jesus and his followers, the early church communities. Love by definition
involves twoness, and three- or four- or more-ness. One
cannot be a Christian alone any more than one can be
married alone. Intrinsic in faith and love is the covenant
of God with God's people, and among the people, in whatever size groups, even in temporary isolation from other
human beings. The eschatological symbols for the con-
summation of human life are the city, the kingdom, the
marriage feast, and the like—communal symbols.

The particular church or local congregation represents
and is the Christian community, despite flaws and minimal
empirical signs of its true nature. The Reformed tradition
has sometimes been weak in a doctrine of the church, but
it has been generally strong in the reality of the particular
community, guided by pastor, elders, and deacons. Of
course, at times it becomes an exclusive club, and at others

a nondescript assembly, but at its best it is a nurturing community. Here teachers can play a critical role.

Mission Oriented

Another topic has been near the surface throughout this discussion. This is the directedness of the church outside itself. A self-contemplating community, a self-serving community, or a self-maintaining community has lost its true mark as a church: a community for others. The nature of love, God's love, in the New Testament is that it descends from God to the human race, and moves outward in space and forward in time, and will be consummated in the eschaton. The movement of love, *agape*, is not directly from God and to God in a kind of return motion. The movement of love, we might say, is down and out! "Down" in creation, in the covenant, and in the incarnation, where God is the origin and the sole mover in the actions of creation and redemption. And "out" toward others, toward the sinners, the needy, the sick and miserable—not only in the present but in the future. "To be reconciled to God is to be sent into the world as [God's] reconciling community," says the Confession of 1967, in a summary of many Bible passages. Again, "The life, death, resurrection, and promised coming of Jesus Christ has set the pattern for the church's mission." This church not merely has a mission but *is* a mission, by its minimal definition. This same confession describes "The Fulfillment of Reconciliation" and sees the comprehensiveness of the mission: "God's redeeming work in Jesus Christ embraces the whole of [human] life: social and cultural, economic and political, scientific and technological, individual and corporate. It includes [our] natural environment as exploited and despoiled by sin. It is the will of God that [God's] purpose for human life shall be fulfilled under the rule of Christ and all evil be banished from [the] creation."

2

Education
for the Public Good

Jack L. Stotts

Gratitude and sovereignty are primary theological categories for Presbyterians. Gratitude to God is the human correlate of that most Reformed of theological affirmations, the sovereignty of God. If we are grateful for being here, trusting in God's sovereignty, we are grateful to God for God's providence in bringing us to this particular place. We rest in the Spirit and are not therefore ultimately restless about our specific location. We do not equate God's providence with our own achievement; we confess that while we are grateful for all God's creation, we also are freed by God's call to be particular agents of God's providence and calling. We are not the entirety of God's chosen vessels. We are one of God's gifts and agents, called to be the Presbyterian church. Gratitude and sovereignty coalesce to enable us, to permit us, to accept our limited role, while trusting that God's provision for God's purpose encompasses more than ourselves.

If that is true, then our task is at once more limited and more demanding. It is laced with humility about who we are, but also it is starched with confidence in God's ecumenical rule. We are freed to say that we are one particular community of faith, with stewardship responsibilities for the fellowship and mission entrusted to us. That steward-

ship includes care for who we have been, are, and will be
through the centuries—past, present, and future. We are
free to ask the limited question of our particular calling.
We can ask: Who are we as Presbyterians?

Let me put that question in the language of anthropol-
ogy: What are our shared values? If we understand the
Presbyterian church to be *an* embodiment of grateful response to God's sovereignty within the larger embodiment
called Christ's church, what is it—or what are the particular values—that makes us who we are and that we have
to contribute to the ecumenical church and to the world?
Let me put it this way: We are part of the one body of
Christ. But what part are we? What are our particular
gifts, our contributions, our distinctiveness? What are the
values that make us Presbyterians?

This idea of shared values has gained both popularity
and credence recently in the analysis of secular organizations. AT&T is a good example. For years AT&T had
one value shared by all its employees: to offer the most
extensive phone service at the least possible cost to all.
Now that value is gone; the crisis at AT&T is to articulate
and embody a new value or values that reflect a new mission.

But who are we? What are our shared values? Others
have attempted to summarize the shared values of Presbyterians. John Mackay's "ardor and order" is a brilliant
example. "Decently and in order" is a popularly recognized summary of who we are. I propose for reflection
that *our genius as Presbyterians is education for the public
good.* A genius here refers to a distinctive value. Its reference is to the guardian spirit of a place, one that marks
it, identifies it, gives it character.

The Genius of Education

One—if not *the*—genius of the Presbyterian tradition
has been its valuing of and commitment to education as

an instrument for faithfulness. If you want to know who we are as Presbyterians—or, more broadly, as members of the Reformed tradition—we are a people committed to education as an instrument for faithfulness. That is our genius. If the Baptists have found their genius in evangelism and church growth, if Anglicans have found theirs in liturgy, then Presbyterians have found their distinctiveness in education.

This education has been in service of the truth, which is itself in the service of goodness. "Truth is in order to goodness," we have said. Thus a mark of the Presbyterian heritage of education is its concern for the public good. Education for the public good was a pennant flown by Presbyterians before it became a secular value incorporated by the modernizing societies of the world.

This genius has been lived out in a variety of institutions: the Sunday school movement, academies, colleges, seminaries, and boards of Christian education. If you want to find out where evangelism was done within the minority communities, for instance, you look to educational institutions. A tremendous number of minority academies and colleges served the task of sharing the good news.

The genius of education for the common good—I want to emphasize the *common* good—is of the essence of the Presbyterian church. This genius has been illustrated by our disputes, by what we fight about. In the nineteenth century the Cumberland Presbyterian Church split away from the dominant Presbyterian church over the question of whether or not there should be educated clergy. The struggle at Princeton Seminary in the 1920s and 1930s indicated the importance in the fundamentalist-modernist controversy of the educational institutions for the identity of integrity of the church. The disputants—all Presbyterians—disagreed on the *content* of education, but they were one on its importance.

Another illustration: What people who are ordained to the ministry of the Word like to be called gives a clue to basic values. Lutherans like to be called "Pastor"; Roman Catholics are called "Father"; Presbyterians love to be called "Doctor!" Doctor means teacher. And Presbyterian ministers don't have offices, they have studies!

The Presbyterian church has at its best seen education for the public good as its genius. That genius has been subject to all kinds of distortions. Education can be reduced to the "academic": that is, abstracted from goodness. Further, education for the public good has been and continues to be, over and over again, corrupted into education for the private good—"the good for me so that I can get ahead." This commitment to education for the public good has also been subject to the attack of anti-intellectualism that is part of the American culture. In the '60s it was the anti-intellectualism of the intellectuals; they saw in institutions the distortions of the goals those institutions were designed to serve, too often being servants of privilege rather than of the public good. But the more virulent attacks have been from the right, from those who would not agree that faith needs understanding and who would limit the role of the mind in religion.

But over and over we have asserted that we as Presbyterians are committed to education for the public good.

Robert Lynn, Vice-President for Religion of the Lilly Endowment, Inc., in a recent address contended persuasively that Presbyterian polity and doctrine have implications for our commitment to education. His reference was to theological education, but I believe its application is broader. Let me quote some paragraphs from his "address" as printed in *The Presbyterian Outlook*, September 17, 1984:

> *Polity* in the American Presbyterian tradition has deep educational implications. This polity presupposes that the quality of congregational life depends upon the work of the Holy Spirit in and through ministers of the Word. In particular, if the ministers of the Word are to be faithful stewards of that Word,

then they should be instructed in as advanced ways as possible in Scripture, theology, polemics, and the life of the Church.

Furthermore, the equality of all ministers requires that the church find some rough way of providing all ministers with approximately the same body of knowledge . . . as advanced as possible, shared with as many people as possible. . . .

The prominent role of elders in the governing of the church also calls for a high degree of literacy on their part; indeed, the extraordinary responsibilities of the ruling elders presupposes a wide-ranging knowledge of both the Word and the world. The Presbyterian attitude toward the elder and toward that office was one of those factors that led our ancestors to be so creative in the establishment of new institutions.

So much, then, for polity. Now let me go on to *doctrine*. In the 19th century, our Presbyterian forebears exhibited a deep passion for Scripture. I can point, for instance, to two people who were on different sides of the war that split the church in the late 1830s: Edward Robinson and Charles Hodge. They were both convinced that the Scripture was the cradle of the Spirit. The New School and Old School Presbyterians were at one on that particular issue.

In this preoccupation with the Bible, the Presbyterians were, in effect, mandating schools. There is a connection between the Bible and schools. A text is something to be interpreted, to be taught, to be learned. That logic begins to suggest a school. . . . The characteristic Presbyterian approach presupposed a liberal arts foundation. The full BA program prepared the seminarian to tackle the history of the textual analysis and to come to terms with the confessional standards of the church.

When that kind of polity is combined with that sort of doctrine, the result is a tribe of human beings who are fascinated with schooling in general and theological education in particular. And that is, I submit, one of the ways of explaining the astonishing number of Presbyterians who were at the heart of educational enterprises in the 19th century. Two quick quotes from E. T. Thompson's book, *Presbyterians in the South*, are accurate and noteworthy—especially when compared to the state of affairs today: "The Presbyterian concern for education manifested during the Colonial period was continued through the early decades of the 19th century; until about 1840 theirs

was the dominant influence particularly in those states where
they had the greatest strength, Virginia, North Carolina, South
Carolina, Kentucky and Tennessee. . . . Wherever the Scots
and the Scotch-Irish settled in America, they started schools.
In this way these Presbyterians did more to start schools in
the South and the West than any other people."

The Word of God

I suggest that it is a primary theological commitment to
the Word of God that has implications for education, polity, and doctrine for Presbyterians. We Presbyterians have
been suspicious of "enthusiasms" of the Spirit and have
focused on the Word as providing discerning power by
which to test the spirits. At times this focus on the Word
has led to aridity and sterility, to "coolness." But we have
been people of the Word. We must be immersed in the
Word (Scriptures), we have believed, in order to discern
and respond to the Spirit.

It is this primary theological commitment to Word of
God theology (in all its forms) that has led us to embrace
education for the public good as a shared value. From
education as shared value has come program and organization and institutions. A certain kind of theology has
led to a certain shared value, which has led to programs
and institutions.

Education for the public or common good as a shared
value for Presbyterians has had programmatic and organizational consequences. From that shared value has flowed
vast energies, energies to shape both church and world.
It has been *a* genius of who we are. "We are a tribe of
human beings" called Christians who share a value of education for the public good. We are who we are as we
manifest and live out of that value. We ignore this genius
at the risk of losing our "souls," our character, our distinctiveness.

And this shared value is not connected with privilege.

It is a gift of God to us, for the whole church and for the world. To claim that gift is to affirm the promise it bears. But if we key in on education as something that is ours by right or is granted for our benefit, rather than being directed toward the theater of God's glory—the world— then the gift becomes a curse. And we shrivel and die.

My proposal for your theological reflection: Out of gratitude to God and with faith in God's sovereignty known through Jesus Christ, we are a particular community with a particular genius. How we define that genius has implications. It is the guardian of our particular heritage. We have shared values over which we are stewards, to empower their power.

One of those shared values—nestled near to the very heart of Presbyterians—is education. And education is not just "book learning." It is connected with, transformed by, faithful action. It is praxis, a reciprocal relation between doing and thinking.

As a tribe of people concerned for education for the common good, we Presbyterians know that the church helps us to discern God's power and presence everywhere. In Alice Walker's novel *The Color Purple*, one of the characters suggests the relation between church and world that is on target for us.

> She say, Celie, tell the truth, have you ever found God in church? I never did. I just found a bunch of folks hoping for him to show. Any God I ever felt in church I brought in with me. And I think all the other folks did too. They come to church to *share* God, not find God.

We share God in many ways. As Presbyterians, one way we share is through education—which is fellowship, which is mutual service, which is upbuilding—for the common good, for the glory of God who is sovereign over all the world.

3

From Here to Eternity: Children in the Church

Mary Duckert

The first day Molly came to church she was eight days old. She had been born at home with the help of a midwife. Her grandfather, a forty-three-year-old cabinetmaker, held her in one capable hand. Her mother, an elementary school teacher, joked with well-wishers in the congregation. "Wouldn't you know our kid's first field trip would be to church?"

This scene might have taken place in 1937. It didn't. The year was 1984. In 1937 the child's grandparents had not been born. But the church in which they stood had celebrated its fiftieth anniversary that year.

Molly was born into history. Because she is a child of the church she will become aware of her history and grow up as a child of the covenant.

In the same month Molly was born, a newborn boy was discovered early one morning by a Roman Catholic sister at the door of a church in Philadelphia. "I heard a noise," she told a newspaper columnist. "I thought it was a lamb." She laughed. "Blimey, he is!"

The child was taken to a hospital, where he stayed somewhere between life and death for a week. The nurses were interviewed, because they had taken "Romeo" to their hearts. "We're expecting great things from him," one woman said. "In another age he wouldn't be with us. He's wired from head to foot with modern miracles. Technology," she added, lest the columnist miss her intent.

"What will happen when he's out of danger?" the columnist asked. "Where will he go?"

"Babies like this don't *go* anywhere," one of the nurses spoke up. "They are *put*. And to answer your question, God only knows."

Romeo was born into history too. His birth made the newspapers and the TV news. But he may never know it. He may know only his present, consumed with staying alive, and eventually his past, a sum of remembered yesterdays. He owes his life, though he may never know that, to a mother who took him to what she thought was a safe place, to a Roman Catholic sister who heard him bleating, to crusty nurses who cheered him on, and to technology.

Both Molly and Romeo are children of the church. Molly will know that and Romeo may, if we who are the church are vigilant and faithful.

They are also children of technology in a way we adults can never be. When we crashed into history in the '20s, '30s, '40s, '50s, and '60s, automobiles, airplanes, television, jet travel, and computers were becoming elements of our culture, but no innovation had yet to claim that it was designed to keep us from dying.

Romeo and Molly are children who very likely will live into the twenty-first century, barring world destruction by technology gone to war. Hans Morevec, a computer scientist from Carnegie-Mellon University, speaks about the "technical possibility" of immortality being developed in the twenty-first century. One of the drawbacks so far, according to Bobby Ray Inman, is that we have not yet learned to duplicate the human brain's complex system of parallel processing. Right now, no matter how big or how fast a computer may be, it performs functions sequentially.

The world of Romeo and Molly is not our world completely. Our past is their past if we incorporate them into

our lives. Their future belongs to them in a way it cannot
to us, because it is dependent upon a present childhood
like none that we adults knew as children.

The Computer Gap

We all grew up in a technological age. Pundits in their
nineties tell of first getting electric power in their homes,
of taking their first airplane rides, of seeing the first talking
pictures, knowing that whatever was new would be re-
placed by something newer. Most of them are beyond
surprise.

Those of us a generation or two younger can appreciate
the vantage point that ninety or more years give an astute
commentator on his or her life and times. We can almost
envy the luxury of watching without being in the daily
business of making a living in a society changing so quickly
by electronic technology.

Sandy Weinberg, professor of computer science at Drexel
University, said in October 1984 that in three months as
much material about computers had been published as had
come out in all the time before. Adults who try to keep
abreast of developments are captivated, confused, or cowed.
Children are growing up in a world where they are affected
by computer science before there is any necessity to learn
about it. They are not—nor can they be—concerned about
the nature of knowledge, the development of artificial
intelligence, or the value of information gathering. The
question of up-to-date hardware and software is either
academic or middle-class. Electronics is not an issue to
Molly, who was introduced in church from her grandfather's hand on her eighth day, or to Romeo, who was
found on the steps of a church, so close to the edge of
existence that he could have rolled off.

The computer gap is more than a difference in what
generations know, think, or accept about this rapidly ad-
vancing aspect of technology. At issue is our identity as a

people who are in charge of a present and in possession of a history intended to be passed on to future generations. There is no absolute reason that developments in computer science must separate generations to the point of depriving the future of its past. But the separation may already be a fear of those middle-class parents and educators who are accustomed by now to learning from "professionals" in college, in weekend workshops, and on floppy disks. We have become absorbent consumers, no longer able to trust what and who we are with our children and our students. We are depriving ourselves of our own legacy—that of being rooted people with citizenship in no less than the kingdom of God. If technological advancements are holding us captive, finding us confused with their mercurial existence, or leaving us cowed and powerless to create, appreciate, and make value judgments on our own, we may already be victims of the computer gap. We have lost the authority given us in our humanity by the grace of God the Creator.

The Humanity Gap

We are twentieth-century rich young rulers. The encounter of Jesus with the rich Jewish leader is in all three Synoptic Gospels. The man asks about his ultimate future, "What must I do to inherit eternal life?" Jesus answers in the language of his and the man's past, "You know the commandments," to which the ruler answers, "Teacher, all these I have observed from my youth." Then Jesus, Mark writes, "*looking upon him loved him*, and said to him, 'You lack one thing; go, sell what you have, and give to the poor, and you will have treasure in heaven; and come, follow me' " (Mark 10:17–21, author's emphasis).

We have been called in words from our past to take on the work of the church as brothers and sisters of the poor. We are called in this day, in this age, to teach, support, and give food, clothing, and shelter to the children of this

day and age. Do we define "children" as the Mollys in
our midst? In five years that child will be in a public school
where she can learn to "write" life stories on a small computer that will correct her spelling and furnish synonyms
when words fail her. Already the Christian education committee of her church is concerned about the children in
the church school being "bored" without "new technology." Her mother learned about computers for young children's education in college: "Sure, we use them in school.
They shortcut here and there, and they're becoming more
useful. But there is very little valuable software for young
children." Molly's mother and father do not have a computer in their home. They predict that they will not have
one for Molly. Molly's father is manager of a home computer store.

Where is Romeo likely to meet the church at work?
How will he learn in five years to tell life stories? What
will they be? Who will teach him of his past? Who will
give him theirs?

We in the church are at a familiar fork in the road. One
tine leads to a well-defined, conscientiously prepared program for believers and their children; another tine leads
toward all of us in the church going in the direction of the
oppressed with our Scriptures, our money, and our technology. This fork is different from those we've hit before.
In choosing life for "our own," we widen the gap between
the "haves" and the "have nots." If the middle-class churches
serve only their own children with what we call "limited
funds," the poor will be not only an underclass but people
surrounded and affected by technology with *no way* to use
it to their advantage. And the church's decision will be
part of the reason for their being where and how they are.
That decision will affect the world.

The Bridge to Somewhere

Christian educators have been forever building bridges
between the child and the church, the home and the church,

the church on the corner and the church in the world, the child and the minister, the young and the old. Now it is time for us to use an old bridge. The rich young ruler reminds us that when we ask the ultimate question, What must I do to inherit eternal life?, we are by our own question assuming we have a past from which to inherit it! Whether we are the prodigals coming home or the older siblings who were always faithful, we ask our question knowing the answer is from the Book of the church.

This time, when it comes to the question of bridges, we might well want to build a new one—or, worse yet, think we have to. It has already been built. But the only way to cross that bridge and hear the good news—*or* the bad news—of the gospel is to get rid of whatever we have that separates us from other people, so that we are brothers and sisters in ministry.

Jesus told the man with riches what to do with them in order to have eternal life. That act would take care of his eternal life, which would not, of course, take care of the rest of his life on earth. "Follow me" took care of that.

Our problem as Christians has always been putting our money anywhere near the voice of Scripture telling us how, indeed, we inherit eternal life. There are Christians in Spanish Harlem or in the *favela* in Rio de Janeiro who could not understand any of this essay, even if it were printed in Spanish or Portuguese. We have never, nor has society in general, dealt successfully with the problems of poverty.

Most of us have not walked on the bridge Jesus offered the rich young ruler. It was not a new bridge then. Jesus spoke as a Jew to a Jew. We are challenging one another in the church today to go the length of the bridge. Christian educators who decide to build other bridges will do so. Read Joshua 24:15 before you try.

4

What Curriculum Is—
and Is Not

D. Campbell Wyckoff

At a meeting of a curriculum consultation committee, sparked by an action of the General Assembly of the Presbyterian Church (U.S.A.) and attended by representatives of various Presbyterian and Reformed bodies, we were asked to address ourselves individually to the question: What educational programs do you want to see in place in your denomination in 1990? I want to keep that question in mind as I deal with a related question: What is curriculum for church education—and what is not?

Curriculum Is a Plan

The curriculum of Christian education is the church's systematic plan for fulfilling its educational ministry. Clearly it is not the whole enterprise. Much of what is most significant goes on in unplanned ways in congregation, family, neighborhood, community, school, and among friends. But it is inconceivable that the church would proceed without a plan that grows out of its faith, its life and work, the persons involved, and the educational process. Most often the plan is more than instructional, having a nurture component (the development of the Christian life) and a vocational component (training for discipleship). Furthermore, the plan is usually seen as involving persons throughout their life span. To implement the plan, programmatic and administrative means are devised and built into the church's institutional life.

Through the years, the Protestant denominations in North America have achieved a remarkable degree of common understanding about curriculum design and development. These understandings are articulated in, though not confined to, such studies as those of denominations in the decades from 1940 to 1960 (by Smart, Hunter, Shinn, Gilbert, etc.), the Cooperative Curriculum Project of the National Council of Churches, and the Stance Paper of Joint Educational Development, with its educational intentions and its identification of theological and educational assumptions. Sources of our understanding are also found in secular literature, as for instance in *Curriculum: An Introduction to the Field*, edited by James R. Gress and David E. Purpel (McCutchan Publishing, 1978), and in *Curriculum Theorizing: The Reconceptualists*, edited by William Pinar (McCutchan Publishing, 1975), with its challenge to the Tyler rationale by advocates of "transcendence" (Philip Phenix), "consciousness raising" (Donald Bateman), and a more existentialist view of educational experience (Dwayne Huebner and Pinar himself).

One of the tasks of any curriculum enterprise is to articulate its perspectives on that common understanding, lest, on the one hand, it try to "reinvent the wheel" or, on the other hand, lapse into a shallow pragmatism and consequent inadequacy.

A new curriculum enterprise is called for when new opportunities and challenges emerge, or when experience with existing curriculum shows up inadequacies—as in the case of curriculum that ignores developments in biblical studies or the church's social commitments—or points to new ways, as in the curriculum of the Uniting Church of Australia. A new curriculum enterprise is also called for when it becomes evident that an existing curriculum is not maintaining acceptance by the church. Caution is advised, however, to be certain of the discovery of the particular causes for decline in use. The new enterprise must address itself to real rather than to hypothetical problems. Valuable common understandings are not to be jettisoned, for instance, because of self-fulfilling theories of cyclical obsolescence or because of generalized assumptions that "everything has changed" or that "we live in an entirely new world."

Although curriculum as educational plan is not the whole picture, it is an essential part of the picture. Our present understanding of the various aspects of the church's life and work is that they are dynamically interrelated and interactive within the whole. Education does not take its place alongside pastoral care, social action, mission, evangelism, stewardship, and the rest, but within a whole that encompasses all of them. Within education the curriculum functions in the same way in relation to other dynamic educational influences, both informal and structural.

Curriculum and Mission

Curriculum, as an educational enterprise of the church, depends upon but is not identical with mission and action. The curriculum is an agent for helping to instruct about mission, to motivate to mission, to reflect on mission, and even to help to determine the character and direction of mission. But mission loses its integrity if it is undertaken for the sake of or primarily within the enterprise of education or its curriculum. Likewise, action is not undertaken for the sake of or primarily within the enterprise of education. The curriculum may—must—serve action, however, in the same ways: instructing about it, motivating to it, training for it, reflecting on it, and as an aid in determining its character and direction. The same kinds of distinctions are to be made in relation to other functions that are integrally related to education and curriculum—worship, evangelism, pastoral care, and the like.

Furthermore, the confusion about religious education, moral education, and Christian education requires study in depth. Their similarities, differences, and varied appropriateness to the church's educational plan need to be determined. At present they are getting more attention in political and scientific realms than in educational or theological ones. They are all strong contenders for our attention, but they often pull in different directions, with few criteria for evaluating and coordinating them.

The Character of Curriculum

A contemporary curriculum may be identified by the character that it embodies and exemplifies and by the functions that it performs. The character of the curriculum is that it does the following:

It locates itself in the living relationship of the church and the person with the triune God, thus seeing itself as a corporate and personal divine-human enterprise. The trinitarian relationships are vitally important. The person and the church sustain direct and indirect relationships with the three persons of the Trinity. Father, Son, and Holy Spirit are active in the enterprise, our awareness of and response to their initiatives being the heart of the matter.

Curriculum also exemplifies the church's social concerns, particularly those for peace and justice. Peace and justice are singled out as particularly important today. They are not intended to preempt the field or to exclude other concerns.

Curriculum focuses on the work, worship, and mission of the particular congregation, embodying what the church is and what it intends and stressing the concept of "the whole church teaching and learning," as in the emphasis of the World Council of Churches on "learning in community."

It incorporates and develops in authentic and dynamic ways the cultures and languages of the people who constitute the church. This aspect of the curriculum is virtually undeveloped; confusion reigns about whether the emphasis should be on cultural specificity or on the multicultural.

Curriculum takes personal and corporate developmental realities seriously. It pays attention to the social needs of individuals and is at the same time alert to the corrective and creative breaking in of the unexpected. This breaking in is both the work of the Spirit and the emergence of significant and natural "turns of events."

The Functions of Curriculum

Curriculum instructs in the essentials of Christian faith and practice, including specific denominational perspectives on faith and modes of practice. By essentials of the Christian faith I mean biblical study, doctrine and theological inquiry, and a knowledge of the church's historical journey. By essentials of Christian practice I mean the disciplines of personal faith, personal ethics, and social ethics and discipleship in and through the church. By instruction I imply the use of the most appropriate selection from the wide range of tested teaching/learning methods available to us—a blend of the didactic, the participatory, the creative, and the technological.

I am concerned that full attention be given both to our ecumenical commitments and to our confessional particularities. We do not become usefully ecumenical by reducing our confessional commitments, but by intensifying them and contributing them dialogically to the whole. Nevertheless, one of our worst blind spots is ignorance of the curriculum scene around the world. Some of the most significant curriculum thinking, for example, is taking place in Germany. Much new curriculum development is taking place in the Third World. In another realm of ecumenism, our failure to establish and maintain dialogue with the Evangelicals—within our own denomination and in other churches—has reached the point of scandal. We know that we have much to learn from them: about writing and editing materials so they will be clear to the user, about attractive products, about marketing, about leadership education. But we are blind to other valuable aspects of their work, such as their astute identification of educational trends, their maintenance of educational vitality, their use of participatory methods, their use of educational technologies, their ways of understanding and using cultural specificity, the integrity of their social concern, and the like.

Curriculum also nurtures the Christian life by making education integral to the church's experiences of worship and the means of grace, fellowship, stewardship, mission, service, and social action; to the church's experiences in the realm of the affective, the aesthetic, and the creative; and to the church's use of study as a means of inquiry, problem-solving, and growth toward maturity in Christ.

Curriculum trains us in identifying significant issues in church and society, in decision-making, and in taking responsible personal and corporate action. Some of these are social issues that we ourselves identify; some are thrust upon us. Training covers biblical and theological reflection on the issues themselves, on the process used to deal with them, and on the results of the action that we take on them. Curriculum as this kind of training is new. It depends upon a differentiated but balanced view of education and action. It is intended to replace mere exhortation to action and cut-and-dried patterns of action. Specific training not only empowers, it goes a long way toward overcoming reluctance to engage in action, and it also does much to alleviate the guilt feelings of the church and of the individual at not being active enough, when what is lacking is skill.

Resources

Present conditions clearly seem to call for the revision and/or replacement of material resources for the church's curriculum. What seems to be required are fewer materials with more permanence and with possibilities of more flexible use. A minimum list would include the following:

• A manual for curriculum planning and selection by the particular church, taking the variety of churches into account and serving the particular church's character and mission, as well as its specific constituency. The manual includes a wide range of options in teaching/ learning experiences and educational resources. It should provide guidance in building and selecting among these experiences and resources to provide a responsible plan and system for the fulfillment of the parish's educational ministry.

• One graded series—permanent but subject to periodic revision—that provides for the needs of children. Included in this series at the upper elementary level is a systematic treatment of biblical design and content, developed to introduce learners to the Bible within an experience of the Word of God.

• A permanent series for youth and adults, providing training in methods of biblical interpretation and comprehensive coverage of the Bible in depth. Also, a series of electives for youth and adults, available at both middle and advanced levels, comprehensive of concerns for instruction, nurture, and training. A prominent element in both series is the equipping of leaders for the various ministries of the church, including its educational ministry.

• A manual for evaluation of the use of the results of curriculum in the particular church, including specific guidance on how to use the findings for the improvement of the enterprise and how to share them with responsible bodies beyond the particular church.

Curriculum Support

One of the most encouraging aspects of the curriculum conference to which I referred in the opening paragraph of this essay was its healthy emphasis on the absolute necessity for thorough, realistic, and continuous attention to marketing, servicing, and leadership training. The commercial reality has become an integral concern. The separation of editors from program people and publishers has to be a thing of the past if resources are to be properly planned, produced, promoted, distributed, used, evaluated, and revised. At every stage all parties must be appropriately and integrally involved.

A minimum set of conditions for servicing, marketing, and leadership training would include:

- A vigorous communication program, designed to inform the church and keep it informed about the specifics of the program.

- A company of trained representatives, deployed in liaison with regional bodies, for introducing the curriculum, interpreting it, troubleshooting on its use, organizing comprehensive and ongoing leadership training, and providing feedback from the field.

- Strategically located resource centers or stores, where resources may be examined, where curriculum counsel may be given to persons and congregations, and where the resources may be ordered or purchased.

- A church-wide company of certified supervisor/trainers whose responsibility is to assist congregations in designing and mounting appropriate leadership training programs.

• A church-wide Fellowship of Christian Teachers, consisting of persons who are trained and certified in the use of the curriculum, who have made specific personal commitment to the educational work of the congregation, and who engage in regular programs of continuing education to update themselves and to increase their effectiveness.

• The production of materials and the maintenance of structures adequate to carrying on and coordinating such a program of servicing, marketing, and leadership training.

5

The Aesthetic
in Church Education

Barbara A. Withers

"Occasionally, we are stilled by lightning," says Maria Harris. "The lightning comes in many forms: a child's smile, a death, a brilliant sunset, a glimpse of skyline, a fragment of music. In each case, however, although the instance differs, we find ourselves in a situation where ordinary knowing slows for a moment, and a different kind of knowing, a kind of not-knowing or unknowing enters our lives. . . .

"Art is one of these ways of knowing. Artistic or aesthetic knowledge develops through our contact with a created form, which shapes and structures human experience literally 'unspeakable' in any other way. Where ordinary discourse and conversation bring knowledge through vocabulary and syntax, with definable and translatable meanings, art—in all its forms—brings knowledge through a simultaneous, integral presentation. An 'all at onceness,' a semblance of life through the vehicle of a *whole*, is characteristic of art, whether the whole offered is a play, a novel, a painting, a cathedral, or a dance." (From the Introduction to *The Aesthetic and Curriculum Development*; Joint Educational Development, 1982.)

Our dream for the future is of holistic church education. Such education will provide opportunities and settings in which learners of all ages will be exposed to and have experiences with a variety of art forms. These media will provide a means both of transmitting and of expressing an aspect of the spiritual life that cannot be touched in any other way. As learners are involved with art forms, they will develop a lasting appreciation of the creative spirit resident in all human beings. But at the deeper level they will have experiences and be enriched in their own spiritual life as well. Responding to works of art will stimulate the creative spirit in their own lives.

The aesthetic has been and will continue to be a valuable tool for imparting an understanding of Christian expression, meaning, and faith to others. And—foremost for the Christian faith and community—the aesthetic is yet another means for God's continuing revelation in our own lives and the lives of others who would be faithful.

Created and Creating

Aesthetic expression is a way for keeping us human. It reminds us that we are created in the image of God and that we ourselves have the capacity for creating. Our understanding of human nature is based on the biblical accounts of creation and on the Great Commandment affirmed by Jesus: "You must love the Lord your God with all your heart, with all your soul, and with all your mind" (Matt. 22:37, TEV). James Luther Adams suggests that the Bible is a great work of art, explaining: "I would say that the characteristic rhetoric of the Bible is indicated by the phrase 'AND IT CAME TO PASS.' . . . And what came to pass? Now you get a story! And these stories are among the great artistic presentations of humanity." (From "Aesthetical Musings: Interviews with Amos Niven Wilder and James Luther Adams," *Religious Education*, January–February 1981, p. 23.)

We become fully human when we are able to integrate both the rational and the nonrational ways of knowing.

The rational mode is dominantly verbal in its expression; the nonrational is primarily *presentational* in nature and concept. In religious education we often focus on the verbal expression in its *discursive* form, to the neglect of the other essential mode of expression—the intuitive, poetic, affective mode. Because we know the great importance of both modes for helping people to become fully human, we recognize that spiritual development depends upon both the discursive and the presentational to be operational in educational environments.

It should be accepted as a firm educational assumption that the aesthetic dimension is important for developing human understanding, communication, enjoyment, and meaning. The aesthetic also opens the possibility for everyone to become part of the ongoing creative process that continually releases the human spirit. As we see creativity in others, we begin to appreciate and discern the creative spirit in our own lives; we sense, develop, and release the gifts we have. In deliberately planned educational experiences, in which we are permitted occasions for looking long and seriously, we begin to develop our own critical, appreciative, discriminating, and creative powers.

Teaching and Learning

Teaching and learning are enriched and enlivened by the inclusion of the aesthetic because such education takes seriously the notion that learning encompasses the whole of human experience. Serious and intentional learning always involves all the senses, but especially the eyes and ears. Looking and listening are primary aspects of learning. Joshua C. Taylor suggests that "to look at a work of art is to think" (*To See Is to Think: Looking at American Art*, p. 7; Smithsonian Institution Press, 1975). It is a thinking that involves the entire person; in both looking and listening we use our mind, perhaps even our heart, and we know from experience that to see and hear is to motivate thinking in us. As we see and hear, so do we think.

We also know that an important part of learning is the opportunity for persons to express feelings. But they also need guided experiences in the presence of the creativity of others. Through the deliberate inclusion of the aesthetic forms of dance, drama, music, poetry, painting, sculpture, and photography, persons are given essential modes for self-expression and also occasions for sharing in the creative expressions of others.

The arts are intense human expressions that can touch and be touched by every person. Because persons are creative beings, the aesthetic dimension can be understood, enjoyed, and created by everyone. Teaching and learning experiences can nurture such understanding and creativity. Of course, essential principles exist for understanding art forms. However, at the heart of helping persons to understand is our effort to help them become sensitive through exposure to a variety of presentational forms and expressions. Jean Mary Morman suggests that a real key to understanding art "lies in learning how to look at, wonder about, question and compare life to art and art to life" (*Wonder Under Your Feet: Making the World of Art Your Own*, p. 1; Harper & Row, 1973).

In developing educational experiences for learners of all ages, educators can help them learn how to be patient in their encounters with the arts. Such experiences can be enjoyable, even exciting. We educators can help learners understand that looking at a painting, watching a film, or listening to a musical composition will take time, patience, and effort. Learners can begin to discover that after time and serious effort such works begin to reveal themselves and their message to the heart and mind. Real understanding of presentational forms has to do with *looking*, often long and carefully; with *listening*, patiently and openly; and with *doing*, engaging in creative activity.

Educators have a unique opportunity for creating an atmosphere for learning that is conducive to experiences with the arts. We can build careful, thoughtful—even critical—looking, listening, and doing into educational procedures and experiences. We want to enable persons to know and to understand that learning to see and hear is a part of learning also to communicate and to speak and to understand—to feel, experience, touch, make contact with the essence of another human being and with that individual's world and experience. It may indeed be true that if persons fail to see and hear the artistic sights and sounds of others, they will fail to develop full and rich human relationships.

To see and hear is to open a new possibility for meeting persons on a different plane; it brings us into contact with a language that only the sensitive and alert can hear, appreciate, and understand. Great artists introduce us to a new world—to a new way of seeing, thinking, understanding, communicating, and believing. Musicians and artists often speak the unspeakable in ways that other means of communicating might not make clear—their struggles, joys, beliefs, ideas, and dreams. Through such sharing the unquenchable spirit of humankind is shared, one with the other. To be cut off from such rich experiences is greatly to reduce the possibility of being fully human. Without help and encouragement, people could miss the opportunities that the arts offer to enable us all to change and renew our view of ourselves and of others. The dreams, hopes, beliefs, aspirations, judgment, and expressions of the human community reside in the arts. The spirit of the living God moves there too—available, approachable.

Claiming Our Heritage

"Christian people have often had a somewhat uneasy relationship with art," Maria Harris reminds us in *The Aesthetic and Curriculum Development*.

Understandably afraid of the tendency to create idols and to enter unfamiliar territory, we have often turned away from art, undoubtedly because of its power to obscure boundaries, to resist final interpretation, and to reveal our *felt* life. At times, the distance we have put between ourselves and the arts has hurt us and, in some instances, impoverished our worship and our education. Because of this uneasiness in some quarters, our liturgies have often been overtalkative and under-ceremonial, with little room for silence and mystery; and our schooling has tended to convey the notion that only the knowing presented as logical, linear discourse has any validity.

In this century we are gradually coming to a chastened understanding, through our biblical studies, that the scriptures we cherish, the Book we cherish, is a book of poetry, of hymnody, of narrative and of drama. We are also realizing in our theology, now become global and thus ecumenical for the first time, that the central Christian themes of creation and incarnation are affirmations of the material universe. The word *aesthetics*, in its most recent meaning, refers to "things perceptible by the senses, things material." . . . It is this material universe of which the author of Genesis speaks: "And God saw that it was *good*."

We must reclaim the rightful place of the aesthetic in our educational practices and resources. The wealth of form and beauty in our power to share belongs to all who would educate, as surely as does the Christian faith and hope we would communicate. In the arts and through human creative expression of the past as well as in contemporary aesthetic expressions and forms, we believe that such faith and hope are often uniquely blended. Through educational experiences with individuals of all ages, we need to take the opportunity to expose ourselves and others to that rich heritage that is ours.

One way we shall reclaim that heritage is to develop open and sincere communication with artists. They can help us to reach that point where we can trust creative expression as a worthy and acceptable vehicle for communicating with one another and with God. Our Puritan forebears were very mistrustful of the arts—not because the arts were considered weak but because they were a powerful medium! The Puritans rejected visual images in favor of verbal statements that they considered to be more manageable and secure. Our challenge is to trust once more the imaginative powers and to equip learners in the church to be more knowledgeable, discriminating, and even judgmental about aesthetic forms and expressions.

As persons begin to understand the arts and as their lives are opened to creative expressions, they will be released to look and listen with both heart and mind when the various media speak their messages. For the arts have power, and it is only as we understand them that we can begin to trust them as faithful modes of revelation. Only then will we put an end to our estrangement of the aesthetic from faith. If we are faithful, we will not retreat from the energies of the arts; we will draw upon them for renewal and change. For we believe in a God of love, truth, and beauty.

Guidelines for Educators

We live in a time of unique opportunity. As it has not been in a long time, the church is open to recovering its aesthetic heritage. We have an opportunity, as educators, to wed the arts to the nurturing life of the church. What follow are guidelines for making that marriage a legal and fruitful one:

• *Seek a balance of ways of knowing* in planning educational opportunities. The aesthetic reminds us that there are a variety of ways of learning, experiencing, and knowing. The ways to the heart are often through the eye, ear, and emotions. Learners need experiences with creative expressions and contact with their aesthetic heritage. These include seeing great works of art, hearing memorable sacred music, and reading significant religious prose and poetry. Learners also need opportunity and encouragement to be creators themselves.

• *Be intentional about incorporating the aesthetic dimension as well as the oral tradition and printed word in all educational resources.* The challenge to those who publish for church education is to discern the partnership between the discursive and the presentational.

• *Recognize that appropriate forms of artistic expression differ at different age levels and should be selected appropriately.* Art forms and expressions from our heritage, as well as those from the contemporary scene, should be chosen in light of the needs, interests, and comprehension levels of learners.

• *Utilize many styles and forms to reflect the wide aesthetic diversity of human creativity.* For example, contemporary art and illustrations, as well as historical art, may be utilized to ask what God has revealed to us, what life has meant to others, what life can be for the child, the young person, the young adult, or adult— and what life is like when lived according to God's promise and plan.

• *Include all elements of the aesthetic in educational resources and opportunities.* A holistic concept of church education requires it. Include color, line, form, word and text, music and sound, texture and feel, fragrance and taste.

• Whether classic or contemporary art forms are used, *provide thoughtful interpretation to guide the learner in fully understanding the intent and message.* The scope of such interpretation needs to be determined by the age level. What is needed is help for learners in looking and listening. They need to be helped to look and listen long enough so that they begin to see the same vision that was part of the artist's original conception or intention.

6

The Reformed Pastor as Educator

James C. Huffstutler

Everyone deserves an identity crisis. Perhaps it is only fair that church education suffered its crisis at the same time as the church itself muddled through one. Much has happened to us in the last twenty years, and it seems that only now are we beginning to realize again who we are as God's church!

For a while it seemed as though we weren't sure we wanted to be the church. We looked around and saw people seeking encounter weekends, therapy groups, alternative life-styles, new sensory experiences—in an effort to find direction for meaningless lives or to heighten the lives they had. The idea of an "afterlife" was considered as something best consigned to the Middle Ages. People were trying desperately to wring out of this life everything they could. So the church sought its direction from the newspaper—or the profundities of the other media. We believed that we had to "listen to the world," forgetting that much of what the world said was not worth taking seriously. Our churches became "centers"; we reorganized communities; we set up therapy groups; we took down our paintings of Sallman's *Head of Christ* and surrounded ourselves with ecology or peace symbols and Coke slogans. Then one day we noticed that other religions and groups bent on saving people were popping up everywhere. We began to wonder if we hadn't ignored a wonderful treasure. Perhaps there was a new need for an old church. Perhaps Moses and Isaiah and Jesus and Paul and Augustine and Calvin had a message for our times.

Pastors were suffering the identity crisis too. We wondered who could possibly get anything from a sermon when there was an electronic revolution going on. Besides, speaking *at* people from a pulpit wasn't communicating; that was a despised model of authority—a parent! We wanted to be adults, not parents. We wanted to be buddies. What was important was hurting alongside hurting individuals. The role of the pastor was far too stereotyped for creativity. Those who were *really* helping people were social workers, counselors, and political activists. Fortunately there were people who remembered that there were once Christians who were loving and truly helpful, unashamed to be pastors—and we felt needed again.

Those days are pretty much behind us. Those of us who have been through them can recall them with an occasional note of humor. Seminaries are filling again; the pastorate is back with a vengeance. There is a new and needed thrust in evangelism; after all, we have to recover some of the ground we lost. Liturgical and homiletical materials are available in great abundance, heralding worship leadership and preaching as nearly lost arts. "Contemporary worship" has put away its carousel projectors, guitars, leotards, and "Morning Has Broken" slide sets, leaving us with the willingness to experiment along with a deep hunger for the rich traditions of truly Reformed—and informed—worship.

An Educational Resurgence?

But what has happened to education? Has it seen a new blossoming? Not yet. And it won't until pastors again see themselves as educators.

The malady may perhaps be characterized by discussions at the General Assembly level. Whereas the Reformed title of "teaching elder" made a critical emphasis, recent discussions have suggested calling pastors "continuing members of Presbytery"—as if that were the way pastors gained their identity! In a bureaucracy, organizational participation and loyalty are the means of identifying faithfulness; God forbid that the church should ever adopt such a model!

Many congregations do little more than give lip service to the educational task of pastors. Pastors know that it is important to teach; they also know that as far as personal survival and development of the congregation goes, there is a great deal of administrative work that must be attended to. Pastors can teach when they've finished all their other work, which, of course, never happens!

Teaching also poses some real ego problems for pastors. Given that there are only so many hours in the week, the time devoted to worship preparation pays off handsomely. But the same amount of time is required to prepare for classes that may touch only a few people. That hurts!

There is also a sense of lofty security when we pastors are in the pulpit. It is to be hoped that we have done good preparation, so that what we say is based on careful study. Still, the feedback from worship is generally exhilarating. We preach for fifteen minutes, and people we have never seen before tell us that we have changed their lives or that they are now able to get through the next week due to our teamwork with the Holy Spirit. How often do we get that kind of payoff from even the best of our classes? If there is a choice between preaching and teaching, pastors generally give priority to the pulpit and let teaching slide.

Time is not an insignificant factor, and good teaching takes a lot of preparation. For occasional classes, there is publicity to be created and distributed; we have to sell classes as cleverly as advertising people sell new products. That becomes demeaning. In a society where millions of

dollars are spent to sell educational materials, we wonder
what kind of novel twist we can put on our description of
a class exploring the social and spiritual abuses of Jerusalem in the time of Jeremiah.

While we are preparing educational experiences of ultimate significance, we find that we are in desperate competition with a plethora of activities from soccer to Jaz-
zercise, with special attention to the current mini-series or
soap on television. Finding a time for educational activities—even for people who beg for them—may be a completely dispiriting undertaking. It seems that there simply
is no good time anymore for education in the church.

There is also a subtle little demon to consider called
"status." In congregations with a multiple staff, why is it
that education is generally at the lower end of the hierarchy
of significant activities? The more successful the pastors
are, the more likely it is that additional staff will be hired
to "relieve" senior pastors of educational responsibilities.
What a terrible model this is for the congregation! Perhaps
it is little different from the example we set in our homes,
where kids go to school but adults are big enough not to
have to learn any longer! Children learn this lesson well:
When you're an adult, it's OK to stop learning.

In sum, pastors don't have to search very far to find
documentation for reasons why they don't do much with
their call to be educators. And this is only a partial listing
of the dragons that live on the battlefield. But beyond the
smoke and fire, there must be a way.

Certainly pastors are not the only teachers in the church.
Therein is a modicum of support for pastors who argue
that they should not be called "teaching elders." That
makes it sound as if they were the *only* teachers. When
one considers church school teachers, youth advisers, and
the many people in a congregation who assume massive
responsibilities for teaching, it might seem arrogant to set
pastors apart in this way. In truth, we should do more to
honor the "teaching gifts" evidenced by all who teach in

the church. But recognizing the educational contributions of other dedicated Christians does not diminish the unique calling of pastors as teachers.

Ordination has a fascinating meaning. It doesn't mean that those who are ordained necessarily have skills possessed by no one else. Rather, ordination is the means by which the church takes some of its own and says, "See here. We need to make sure that certain functions are performed—decently, and in order. We know that others can do them, but when everybody is responsible, then nobody is finally responsible. And we want someone to be finally responsible. So we've chosen you, and given you a holy trust." One of the functions given to those who are ordained is to "keep the mysteries," administer the sacraments. They are also to oversee the worship of the congregation and be pastors to the people. And they are to teach the people; they are "teaching elders." When we look closely at our Reformed tradition, we see that it would be virtually impossible without this teaching function. Even the clergy vestments are academic symbols.

Whether pastors like it or not, they represent the entire congregation. The community looks upon these individuals as the best indicator of what a particular parish represents. And the congregation itself, in that the members have elected the pastor, has said, "This is the person we have chosen and elected to lead us." How critical it is, then, that the pastor, though not the only educator in the congregation, symbolize for the congregation and community the importance of learning in the Reformed tradition.

Education in the Reformed Church

In the thinking of John Calvin, the church did not begin on the road to Caesarea Philippi. Since the church is by definition the gathering of God's people, it began way back in the Garden of Eden! And for Calvin, the Spirit of Christ was very much present even in the earliest such gathering. Church education has always been concerned with telling the story of the faith and setting forth and examining the quality of living, the set of values, that have to do with living in obedience to the Lordship of Jesus Christ. God's people in earliest times were called to this task; it will be no different for the faithful in the future.

Certainly one of the most important aspects of the Reformation was the return to the authority of the Bible. It must be read regularly and respected, and all other authority is subject to it. If the Bible is God's Word, then that Word must be made available to the people. Hence schools (education) became important in order for people to have direct access to that Word, without depending on the interpretation of any other person.

Martin Luther felt that personal reading of the Bible was not enough; the Bible must be proclaimed. When we're off by ourselves, we become pretty good at forcing the biblical meaning to conform to our own interpretation. But something remarkable happens when the Bible is proclaimed and the Spirit enters the listener through that process. Luther, however, would not have the proclaimed word without the study of the Word—as his own teaching activities evidenced. So the Bible becomes much more than a book for the church; it is almost sacramental in that the physical may become the instrument of making present the spiritual God!

The pastor as educator is called to be the "teacher of the book." In worship, pastors have no right to speak other than as those who teach the ways of God made known through the Bible and who exhort people to come to know personally the God whose story is told there.

Another distinctive aspect of church education is the working of the Spirit. Whereas our educational processes may be little different from those of other institutions, and even our subject matter may be taught by others, still we believe that God works uniquely in the education of the church. The church's story remains a story until it becomes enlivened by the working of God's Spirit. In this respect, church education can be compared with no other educational process.

Church education is a community affair. It soon becomes obvious that where people gather to worship their Lord, where the Bible is seen as God's Word, and where adults and children commit themselves to live in obedience to the Lord made known in Scripture, there is a distinct community. The development of a community with this kind of self-awareness is the primary function or mission of the church, commissioned to preach, teach, and serve. An examination of this commission should make clear the requirements placed upon the leader of this community, its pastor. But the community itself, by being a faithful community, also teaches. The congregation sets the tone for energizing learning. It is clear that when the community values church education, it will happen.

All too often, when we think of education we think of a classroom. Classrooms are important—all kinds of classrooms, formal or informal, intergenerational or those that minister to particular ages or needs. However, the session and pastor can make sure that education reaches beyond the classroom to pervade the life of the congregation. The story of the faith can be told in many ways, from quizzes in the order of service on Sunday morning and in the church newsletter to the maintenance and use of a good church library, which makes books, video cassettes, and other materials available to the congregation. Worship itself (Reformation Sunday and other celebrations) reminds us of the faith and of our tradition. There are many such means.

It is also important that the members of the congregation, as well as the session, know what is being taught in the church school. Brief course descriptions in church newsletters enable the members of the congregation to be aware of how their baptismal vows are being fulfilled.

As a pastor and teacher, I have been struggling with an attitude that may be a regional one. It came up in a study with our junior high and senior high Fellowship of the Carpenter. As we were studying the book of 1 Corinthians, we came to some sections that certain of the young people found open to question. (That's a nice way of describing it.) Suddenly I found myself confronted with the following logic:

A: Everybody is entitled to an opinion.
B: Much of religion is not a matter of hard facts but of varying opinions.
C: Therefore one person's opinion is as good as another's.

I discovered that our schools, in encouraging students to come to conclusions, have so promoted opinion formation that some students cannot differentiate between an opinion and an *informed opinion*. Tracing the discovery back, I saw that this disposition develops quite early, and to such an extent that church education is suffering. The feeling of many young people is that there is *nothing to learn* in church education, since it is basically a matter of having an opinion.

This is not something that is found exclusively with youth. A young woman in our congregation decided to marry a young man of the Jewish faith. As they were discussing with the rabbi the implications of a mixed marriage, he asked her if she was sure she knew what she was doing. She replied, "I don't think there's really much difference between Christianity and Judaism." The rabbi sent her back to me. I despaired!

At the time of a funeral, it is not unusual for the pastor to hear about the deceased, how he never entered a church or indicated the slightest religious interest of any sort, "but a finer Christian you'd never hope to meet."

There *is* a content to our faith that is more than uninformed opinions and a generalized goodness. We are not so naive as to suppose that there is no difference between faith and understanding. However, reflection on our faith is essential for growth. Somehow pastors must communicate the fact that an uninformed faith is prey to the flimsiest predator.

Some Cues for Pastors

I cannot help believing that pastors need to be involved at every level of education in the parish, whether they are teaching there or not. To turn all educational responsibilities over to others may be rationalized as "trust," but in the end it is an abandonment of responsibility. A committee may choose the curriculum that the church school uses; the pastor ought to be on that committee—providing not only expertise but support.

Pastors need to be involved in more than administrative support. The pastor who is known only from the pulpit is seldom a pastor who is known. Pastors who occasionally get into the children's church school, who are a part of the youth fellowship discussions, who teach the communicants classes, who work with the women's groups—these are the pastors who know their people and understand their needs.

It should go without saying that pastors themselves should be constantly learning. We start out with a solid academic background, but by the time we complete preparatory training, there is a new job to master and some living to do that might have been postponed during seminary preparation. All of a sudden, we are out of the habit of studying, and nobody requires it of us.

One problem for the pastor-as-learner is the reluctance to probe unexplored areas. We tend to focus on an area of interest and then center all our study around that. We become more expert in an area where we may already be well informed, letting other areas slide. And the longer we are in the pastorate, the greater the tendency to let strong feelings take the place of honest learning.

It is sometimes difficult for teachers to become students again. Some teachers even have difficulty remaining human; omniscience lifts us above the earthly plane. We quickly classify rather than truly discover. We nod knowingly rather than listen honestly. And for some reason, when it comes to church education we are susceptible to the worst forms of faddism; ideas of merit, rather than merely contributing to the educational process, *become* the educational process. For example, if everything must be reduced to behavioral objectives, every understanding is thereby reduced to its most insignificant, but measurable, dimensions. We don't just provide intergenerational activities; we make *everything* intergenerational and scorn anyone who suggests that young people might do best by having their own group or that older people might really have very little in common with the learning needs of small children. Teachers become "learning facilitators" or "educational expediters" or receive some other ridiculous title. We are scared to death of authority; no one is in charge because everyone is in charge. Lectures are poison; inductive learning is the only valid way of learning, even when there is nothing within the student to induce! There was a time when church educators were real innovators, but lately they've been looking for another bandwagon to climb aboard.

The best way for pastors to get past faddism is to be good students themselves. Study what is current, but also study the classics. And always ask, "Is what we're trying to do here consistent with our understanding of the gospel?"—or, more crassly, "Would Jesus have felt like a fool doing what we're doing or saying what we're saying?"

One of the tasks of the pastor-as-educator is maintaining the spiritual dimension. Our church constitution wisely requires a prayer to open and close our meetings. Practically, we may feel that such prayers often do little more than get people to be quiet, but in actuality they do much more: They remind us that we are God's people, subject to the Lordship of Jesus Christ. It is the task of pastors to remind congregations what we are about, what our commission pertains to. We need to remind those who serve—from those who work in child care right up to those who provide transportation for senior citizens—that the working of the Holy Spirit is what enables us.

To the End of the Century

As Reformed and reforming Christians, as those who consider the role of the pastor to be an educator, what can we suggest as we consider the shape of education to the end of the century—and beyond? Certainly there is new technology to be considered, and there will be more on the way. Computers, tape recorders, video cassettes, copy machines, and quick-print facilities have already made an impact on the ways we teach. The terms "politics," "hunger," "poverty," "ecology," "peace," "freedom," and "equality" suggest concerns that the church must also address. Few congregations would be willing to provide a room for computers when there are people in the neighborhood who are freezing or starving. Methods and the pressing considerations of the moment are important, but are there some basic understandings that will define the work of the pastor as educator? I would suggest the following.

I sense that we think church education of the future will be futuristic. I suspect that little of it will be! We will still have some great teachers who use old cardboard boxes for bulletin boards and whose students learn the facts and the feelings of faith. We will also have some classes where the students are hooked up to all kinds of gadgetry and will learn little more than how to operate the equipment. *It is important for us to remember—and to teach—that as*

well as having a future, we have a tradition. Understanding
that tradition will possibly be the best provision we can
make for decisions that can only be made tomorrow.

Recently I had the opportunity to take a study leave at
a local seminary. First came the shock of getting back into
academic vocabulary and coming to terms with some of
the "groupthink." (For instance, I soon came to realize
that in seminaries, everything must be "viable.") I selected
a seminar on John Calvin; I had studied Calvin in my
earlier seminary training, but I had never taken an entire
course on his theology. A thrill came over me as I realized
that I was now mature enough to be able to deal with those
parts of Calvin with which I might not entirely agree without feeling I had to dismiss him completely. I also liked
the fact that I didn't need to make Calvin *relevant.* I just
wanted to see how he handled things in the sixteenth century. I also wanted to know how he stood up to Luther,
since, as a Presbyterian, I had always been a little em-
barrassed about my preference for Luther's dash and style.
How surprised I was to find a theology that made sense
to me. And the issues with which Calvin dealt were not
irrelevant to our age: Calvin had Protestant refugees fleeing
into Geneva, putting a strain on its economy, in the same
way that we had the Asiatic boat people coming into ours.
In our post-Watergate age, I found Calvin addressing the
question of support of a political leadership when that
leadership was corrupt. Calvin wrestled with the handling
of new ideas that the people found threatening—much as
I do. What could have been more threatening to the status
quo than the Reformation itself? I had thought I was going
to read a period piece. Instead, I found tremendous direction for my own life and ministry. I suggest that the
great thinkers and saints of the church have as much to
say to the future as even our best contemporary theolo-
gians—who also must be heard and appreciated.

There are many views of the future. Which will we buy
into? There are many options for living. Which have we

chosen? *As Christians, we are different; we must never forget this.* Our society will tell us what the future will be like. Each week we can find an article in the newspaper predicting how everyone will live. But Christians have never lived as everyone else has lived, and I suppose it will be no different in days to come. In one respect, we live in the light of God's future; in another respect, we create our own future. A third future will be that which the world creates, to which we will be called to minister. The best we can do is to seek to influence that future as it is developing and then offer whatever service we can to situations as they arise.

I'm not much of a futurist. I would rather work faithfully and well now with what I've been given. Certainly there are some things ahead that I cannot foresee. Sometimes I can foresee but can do little to change them. In the Sermon on the Mount, Jesus told his followers not to worry about life's incidentals. Take care of each day as a good steward; tomorrow is today's fruit, and all is part of the providence of God.

Church education must make us intimately familiar with what God has done with God's people through the ages. But no understanding of our past will ever remove the freedom of God's Spirit to astound us, making the impossible possible. If we as educators can only get our people to look around and discover even now the wonder of God, then the future will not be too much for us.

7

Issues
of Leadership

Freda A. Gardner

On what basis does anyone or any group dare to predict what may be true fifteen years from now, much less how it will be for another century? Over the past several decades we have learned, slowly and sometimes painfully, to question those who predict, those who describe, those who prophesy. We know to ask about age, social and economic status, values, biases, and the like. We have come to realize that predictors, describers, and even prophets can shape that which they purport to be located in the future. We know that all which can be examined and evaluated may be viewed from a broad range of perspectives and through a variety of lenses, that the purpose of the examination itself shapes what is to be found and made public. How then do we, individually and as a denomination, dare to say what will be so in the future?

The Mind of Christ

We dare precisely because of who we are, in all our diversity, in all that distinguishes us from one another and from all others. We dare because we are part of an always reforming church called into being and sustained by an eternally creating and redeeming God. We dare because we confess that the results of our work must be brought under the scrutiny of that God and our perception of what that God is about, even as we would rest from the labors that brought our work to fruition. Our loyalty as members of the Reformed body of Christians is to none other than Jesus Christ. It is to discern the mind of Christ that we constantly turn in any situation, even those which we help to create and in which we both exult and confess. For years a burden of the church and of its educational ministry has been the illusion that we can say with finality what we are about. If there is any finality, it is reflected in our recognition that saying who we are as the body of Christ in the world is the work to which our vocation points us. When we say yes to God's gift to us in Christ, we say yes to a lifetime of seeking after our place in the mind and the ministry of Christ. Christ's mind is not won by our successes but given as the essential for our faithfulness.

And so we as a church and each of us as individual members of it dare to say that it seems like this to us. It seems that God is about the same business that has been the agenda from creation. It seems that God is empowering the church to see in the present situation that which is of God and that which threatens to impede God's purposes. It seems that the church is still to be, in its members and in its life of service, what Letty Russell calls the "as if" of the coming reign of God throughout the whole created order. It seems that the life of the church is shaped by its continuing responsiveness to God's revelation and empowerment—and in all of that is described the purpose of Christian education.

That education is an important ministry in our church appears on the surface to be beyond debate. At one level, evidence abounds to support the significance we attest to when we affirm an educated clergy and laity. Church budgets, denominational colleges and curriculum, buildings and renovations, education support staff at the national level—all these and more suggest that we do indeed see education as primary. But there is, perhaps, equal evidence that such is not the case. When budgets are cut in congregations, the education program is likely to suffer first. When staff must be reduced, it is the educator who is often the first to go. Curriculum choices are frequently made on utilitarian bases rather than on educational criteria. Programs of education are brought in from outside the denomination because they are attracting people and not because they are consistent with what the church or denomination says about itself. Education is kept manageable by our seeing it only in terms of children or only as a specific program, not as intrinsic to the life of discipleship.

The Purpose of Leadership

If it is agreed that Christian education is an aspect of the church or a dimension of the mission of the church, then all that the church is and does to live its life in response to God is the context and primary shaper of the educational ministry. Just as the church lives by discerning what God is about in its midst, so the educational leadership seeks to participate in that process of discernment. Indeed, it is the fundamental task of education to discover appropriate means for such discernment and to help others to develop the sensitivities and skills to engage in it. That is an ongoing task. It is not something to be done once or every five years or every time a new pastor is called or every time a new denomination is formed. These may be especially appropriate times for many reasons, but they are times among many times. The task of discerning what God is about in order to participate with God's activity for the world God created and is redeeming is at least half of what the life of discipleship is all about.

The other half may be described as acquiring the knowledge and skills and discipline to engage with God in that activity. In a connectional church such as ours, everyone is responsible for getting that work done. Not all, however, must be engaged in exactly the same way. Calling out the gifts of individuals, congregations, and governing bodies, and supporting the exercise of those gifts on behalf of the church for God's world, is a vital aspect of the educational task. Likewise, we are called to witness to God's activities by affirming and supporting those outside the church who call themselves by other names but who work at attending to and tending the world. This responsibility belongs to us who confess that we have not captured God in our belief system or in our church structures but, rather, worship and serve a God who establishes a kingdom by any means consistent with the characteristics of that kingdom, using workers and their efforts for peace and justice wherever they may be found.

The Source of Leadership

Leadership in Christian education is as varied in its source as it is in its purpose, as diverse in its style as it is in its motivation. The last decades have seen an increase in the number of employed persons functioning in leadership roles in education, an increase in the number of ordained persons whose position descriptions have been primarily focused on education, an increase in part-time education positions filled by lay people who have been trained in the congregation and perhaps through the support of education programs sponsored by middle governing bodies. It also appears that in the last twelve or fifteen years women have been increasingly reluctant to emphasize educational ministry in their seminary education programs and have developed other gifts and skills for ministry in order that ordination would not lead them automatically to that one arena in the life of the church where it has been acceptable for women to work.

Fear of stereotyping has meant that many women have denied their substantial gifts for teaching and administering. Many men have accepted forms of ministry for which they never prepared and from which they seek escape as soon as their dues in a first call have been paid. On a more positive side, the last decades have seen the growth of associations of professional educators, which include more men committed to making education their primary form of ministry and more women eager to develop into professionals, seeking to hold themselves accountable for the work to which they are called. Among such professionals, standards and procedures, certification and accreditation, ordination and relationship to the larger church have been in the forefront of discussions.

Political realities cannot be ignored. Congregations want different forms of educational ministry and different leadership for those ministries. Pastors want and expect different competencies and different working relationships with staff members in education. Christian educators who are not educated for that profession are vulnerable in the extreme to the whims and vicissitudes of pastor and parish. Christian educators with theological education but without ordination are almost equally vulnerable. Salaries for educators are often determined on the basis of sex and lay or clergy status rather than on education and experience. There is another vulnerability for those who do not have a theological education: their inability to judge the fads and trends, the packaged promotional materials and "quick fixes" for program problems that come flooding into the church. Gearing themselves up to learn and perform in the latest way guaranteed to increase attendance or promote the Bible or win youth for Christ or keep the family together, they have little knowledge with which to evaluate and less with which to defend their programs in relation to the nature and mission of the church or in relation to the goals of a particular congregation or senior minister.

Leadership in the church's ministry of education can be viewed from so many perspectives that one could well imagine any preconceived notion of that leadership could be affirmed if the right perspective was chosen. The church has done just that in both theory and practice. If leadership is seen to be teaching, the church raises up teachers; if leadership is managing, then managers are found or produced; if leadership is enabling, then those who enable are named church education leaders. A visit to no more than a few congregations will probably reveal a variety that the preceding sentences only hint at. A Sunday church school teacher becomes the church school superintendent and soon is making all decisions of an educational nature. An interested parent introduces a resource to a congregation and is given carte blanche to use it again. A good discussion leader becomes the one who chooses all the topics for adult education and sets the standards for what makes a good adult class. A pastor with gifts in counseling soon has everyone in the congregation seeing learning as therapy, and small-group sessions become the norm. Someone who thinks that the church is to be "out there" undercuts formal study and makes hands-on activity the only mode of discipleship growth. A public school teacher, appalled at the lack of biblical knowledge at all age levels, sets up an academy of learning with courses and credits and tests and promotions. The reflective and evaluative dimensions of church education are ignored or seen primarily as rating success in terms of expediency and proximate goals.

Issues for the Future

What will be the issues and circumstances that determine leadership in our church in the years to come? I suggest that there are three of fundamental significance. These may be proven to be secondary to some that I do not see at the present. However, I believe that these will have to be reckoned with by the church, by our seminaries, and by our governing body staffs, as well as by those who feel called to ministry leadership within the church.

The first is the issue of ordained and lay professional leadership. In spite of the protests that come from all sides, there exists a hierarchical ordering of the church and of ministry. There is little to suggest that this will change without some disciplined effort, some confession and repentance, some forgiveness, and a great deal of acceptance of new responsibility. In his book *The Church* (John Knox Press, 1984), Wallace M. Alston, Jr., discusses ministry and the misunderstanding of *diakonia* as office instead of service. Drawing on the insights of Emil Brunner, Alston asserts that "once it is claimed that certain people are established in office by God, a divinely ordained ecclesiastical structure emerges wherein certain people wield power by divine right; and a cleavage is opened between clergy and laity which was never intended in the apostolic church." He says, further, that "the distinction between ministries, and between the ministry of all and the ministry of Word and sacraments, is one of function, not one of theological preeminence or spiritual superiority."

Although there are presently a number of significant movements related to the ministries of the laity, our church has a long way to go in translating what it *says* about those ministries into what it *does* to encourage, support, and respect them. Lay professional leadership in Christian education is neither evaluated nor recognized nor rewarded by the same criteria used for ordained leadership. Length of a seminary program is often the basis for calling a person to a position and paying that person on a particular salary scale. Particular course work and field experience are frequently secondary to the degree conferred. Continuing education requirements, similar to those that attempt to build in professional accountability for clergy, are not established by the church for its lay professional leaders. They must create such standards and accountability for themselves.

These realities are a partial explanation of the recent effort by the former Presbyterian Church U.S. and now by the newly reunited Presbyterian Church (U.S.A.) to create a fourth office of ordination, the office of Educating Elder. While such an office would support women and men who cannot seek ordination to the Word (and sacraments) without sacrificing their integrity, a fourth office raises questions that the church cannot ignore. For instance, there are others in the church who already have a theological education—or would gladly submit themselves to a seminary degree program—who would be ready and eager to promise the church that they would bring biblical and theological reflection to bear on their various occupations, both inside and outside the church. Such persons might also wish to be set apart by ordination for their ministries. On what basis will they be denied? How do those of us committed to education in the church teach the doctrine of vocation, the doctrine of the church, the Reformed understanding of ministry—and then deny to others what we claim as our right?

Sometime the church is going to have to do some hard work again in establishing consistency between what it teaches and what it does in these areas so vital to the ordering of the life and ministry to which we have all been called. The setting of standards for grievance procedures, for support policies, and for rights and responsibilities cannot proceed in any really helpful way until the fundamental questions of ministries and functions, of the role of education and accountability to the church, have been faced and adequately addressed theologically and politically. It is a task that must be undertaken by the church and not by Christian educators alone.

Second is the issue of the particular and peculiar needs for leadership of particular and peculiar congregations and other church bodies. It is quite apparent that not all congregations need—or think they need—the same kind of educator. Some churches want program developers, some want managers, some want enablers, some want expert teachers, some want overall administrators, some want resource consultants. The list could be lengthened by a simple survey of the congregations of any one presbytery and broadened by asking after the needs of middle governing bodies, mission schools or programs, agencies, colleges, and seminaries. To be sure, not all of what the church in its various forms says it wants requires a formal seminary education. But everything asked for requires one or more persons to take responsibility for what is *not* asked for and yet still must be attended to, if the church is to be faithful to its educational responsibility.

If pastors want program managers, then pastors must do the theological reflection on the programs, must raise the questions of consistency and integrity, must lead the congregation to recognize that the way we educate teaches as much as what we call the content of our teaching. A theologically trained Christian educator should do all those things; if a person not so trained is called to the job, someone must fill in the gaps. In the congregation that someone is the pastor. If congregations want enablers, then pastors must be the theological teachers who remind both the enabled and the enabler that gifts are given with a purpose having to do with Christ's mission in the world and that accountability is the other side of gift. If church-related colleges want good teachers of subject matter, then deans and presidents must accept the responsibility for shaping the faculty so that the witness to the gospel is embodied in those who teach with the diversity and inclusiveness that teaches as much as course content.

Filling a gap in whatever is perceived as the educational ministry is simply not enough. The work that is done by the layperson raised up from the congregation, by the public school teacher brought in to direct the curriculum choice and teacher education, or by the group facilitator who is employed to nurture small groups must be done in a context that includes serious biblical and theological study and reflection. That study and reflection must focus, in part, on the work of the paraprofessional, just as it would be held as essential to the work of the ordained or lay minister or the director. The primary responsibility for such effort—in the absence of a theologically educated church education specialist—falls to the pastor, who is the church's primary educator. The implications of this for seminary education suggest new questions to be asked and answered as seminarians prepare for ministry as well as new dimensions to the standards by which the church evaluates and affirms readiness for ministry.

The third issue, prompted by the second and by the economic conditions that prevail today, *is support of the educational ministry by the larger church.* While some congregations seem quite able to provide all the resources of personnel and material that a responsible education program requires, more and more are faced with limited budgets and with fewer people who have or will take time for leadership. Without access to resources and without professional leadership to adapt available resources and create alternatives when such are not available or accessible, church education suffers. Resource centers, which make available programs and people as well as materials, must be developed in a far greater number than we have seen thus far and in much richer depth and scope than has been the case in general.

Who does the work of helping people to grow in faith, and in the understanding of what that faith means for life, is not the most important question. In our tradition, *all* people are called to involve themselves in that task. It is God who gives us faith and God's Spirit who works in us and among us to nurture and shape that faith. But as is true in all human endeavor, well-meaning people often work at cross-purposes with God's Spirit. There is also the tendency of people to let everyone's work become no one's. Someone or some persons must take responsibility for faithful living in the midst of learning, for making the traditional resources of the church available and under-standable, for supporting the risks that must be under-taken if God's Word to us is to become God's Word and love for the world. Although all are called to be theolo-gians, some must be equipped to lead the church in the process of ongoing study, reflection, and action, which instructs the church, disciplines the church, and empowers the church to witness to the gospel in the world.

8

The Church
and Young Adults
Mary Paik

When we speak of young adult ministries, we usually have in mind a grown-up version of youth ministries. Many church people can't—don't—distinguish a "youth" from a "young adult." They all look alike because they all look "youngish." However, ministry with young adults is vastly different from youth ministry in its shape and content. Different needs and concerns arise for those who are between the ages of eighteen and thirty-five than for senior high youth.

The term "young adult" itself has been subject to criticism and misunderstandings. To some, the term implies folks who are not quite adults yet; others feel that the term connotes the upward mobility of those who are just getting started in life in terms of economy, stability, and power. The Presbyterian Church (U.S.A.) has defined the young adult category as including the ages from eighteen to thirty-five. This is a wide range; one hardly expects an eighteen-year-old to have the concerns, needs, life experiences, or maturity level of a thirty-five-year-old.

The age span of eighteen to thirty-five is one during which most young adults face many "first time" experiences: They may move away from home for the first time, get married, have children, go to college, make career decisions, enter the professional world, find full-time jobs, or enter the military. Because of this extremely broad diversity in experience, as well as the variety of subsequent needs and concerns, many people would claim that "young adults" is not really a legitimate category for ministry. Nonetheless, the category exists, as there are sufficient observed commonalities among young adults in the United States upon which educational ministry may be based.

A Baskin-Robbins Society

In his book *Megatrends*, John Naisbitt explores ways in which our society is restructuring itself. He calls today's society the "Baskin-Robbins Society," where we are faced with multiple choices in everything from models of cars to designer fruits and vegetables. Young adults are faced with countless life-directing decisions in an almost zoolike society.

A college student reflects: "I entered college thinking that I wanted to get a well-rounded education. But I realized during my second year of college that a well-rounded education will not get me a job after graduation. So I changed my major to computer science. I don't think this field fits my personality, nor does it bring me much personal satisfaction, but I have to think about my future. Even in the field of computer science, the competition is pretty stiff. I spend all my time with my schoolwork—so in a sense I am spending all my time doing something that really doesn't fit my personality or bring me much personal satisfaction. I hope that all this work will pay off in the future. But the irony of it all is that some are calling the late '80s the dawning of the new Renaissance, so therefore there will be a need for a new 'Renaissance person.' I really don't know what to think anymore. I can't change my major again because I've almost completed my degree. I only want a decent job after graduation."

A lawyer comments: "I thought I would be married by

the time I turned thirty. Well, I will be thirty next month, and I don't think I am going to make it. I reveled in the educational and professional opportunities open to me as a woman, and I didn't want to waste those opportunities. So I trudged on and on, wanting to be successful. I guess I didn't have time for marriage. I think one never 'has' time for marriage in our society. I think one 'makes' time for marriage. In any case, at thirty, it's difficult to find a man who isn't threatened by my professional status. I think most men with whom I come in contact don't really know how to treat me as a lawyer and a woman. They usually ignore one or the other. Because the sexual roles aren't well defined anymore even in dating situations, it can get pretty complicated, often humorous—after the fact, of course. I am glad that more women are choosing to have babies after thirty. That's good news for me, because I don't want to be alone all my life. I think the women who are in graduate schools now are giving much thought to the whole issue of the importance of having both a family and a career. Perhaps they won't be so starry-eyed about professional status as the women in my class were. I sound and feel archaic when I think about the 'new generation' of professional women in graduate schools! Perhaps I've already become archaic in this rapidly moving society."

A junior high school teacher says: "I really enjoy teaching, and I think I'm good at it. But the only reason I can be a teacher is that my wife makes almost twice as much money as I do. I never thought I'd be in this position when I was growing up, but it has worked out well for both of us. We both enjoy our jobs very much. The only thing we don't like is that we've had to make two major moves based on my wife's career. We are now two thousand miles from our respective families, and I don't like the fact that we are so far away, especially for our children. I wanted them to have constant contact with the extended family the way I did. I want my children to have a strong sense of cultural and ethnic identity. I am not sure how to do that without the help of the extended family. My wife and I hope to move back in the near future—but that would mean another move for the children."

The Church's Role

What is the role for the church with young adults who live in this highly mobile, quickly changing, very competitive and complex society? Perhaps an initial response is to ask, "Is there a need for ministry with young adults in the church?" Some people observe that since most young adults have left the church, there is no need for young adult ministries until they come back. Others say that the role of the church should be to get these young adults back. A fruitful starting point, perhaps, is to explore why there are so few young adults remaining in the church.

Many young adults shy away from involvement in the church either because of their past experience or because of a stereotypic image of the church. Kevin, who is a researcher, recalls: "I stopped going to church when I left home for college. I never stopped believing in God, but I couldn't make sense of the stories learned in Sunday school. What do Moses, David, and Jesus have to do with my life today? That was a nagging question in the back of my mind, but I never could ask anyone seriously. All the religious folks on campus never seemed to have any doubts, while most of my friends didn't think about religion at all. After I graduated from college, I wanted to go back to my church, but I realized that I couldn't. Most people at the church still referred to me as Mr. and Mrs. Chang's son and could not see me as a responsible adult. I still have some questions about my faith, but from what I have experienced, I doubt that the church is the place where I can struggle with those questions."

Linda, a seminary student, says: "I am amazed even now at the negative connotation the words 'minister' and 'church' have for a lot of people. I guess the media have played a big part in this stereotyping of churches and ministers. I think the media paint a picture of the church as a place where people go on Sunday mornings to hear about how 'bad' they've been all week, while the minister is a person with a holier-than-thou attitude who imposes strict moral codes and makes people feel guilty. Other people have had experiences where religious people have tried to convert them too enthusiastically, so they stay away from churches altogether. As a person entering the professional ministry, this misconception bothers me very much."

Paul, who is a cabinetmaker, recalls: "Whenever I think about the church, I remember my fourth-grade Sunday school teacher who used to make me feel awful about not having my Bible verse memorized. I hated going to church as a child because I always felt like I was never good enough to be a Christian. I know it's not fair to judge the whole church based on my fourth-grade Sunday school experience, but I can't help it. I just don't like the way the church makes me feel."

Like Paul, many young adults realize that it's not fair to judge the church based on their limited experience or on media stereotypes; unfortunately, however, very few ever get the opportunity to change those views. If nothing else, the church must be an environment where young adults can process their past experiences with the church and be allowed to explore what adult faith might mean. When the church becomes an arena where critical thinking is encouraged, it can then foster the discovery and the rediscovery of what lived-out personal and corporate faith can be.

Need for Community

For the church to be a place where discovery and rediscovery of the faith occurs, it needs first of all to provide a sense of community for young adults. According to John Naisbitt, the traditional definition of "family" (father, the breadwinner; mother, the caretaker of house; and two children) is changing; now it often includes the important relationship between people not tied by blood or marriage but by voluntary association, such as unmarried couples, close friends, and group houses. Additionally, one out of every four is a single-person household. Given these changes in family life patterns and given the highly technological society in which we live, young adults feel a strong sense of need for community. Today's young adults don't need more programs from the church. Anyway, the church can't compete with the slick, fast-paced world in inventing programs. Rather—and this is true especially for singles—there is a vital need for the church to provide a loving, caring community of people where young adults will be accepted.

When the church creates a "singles ministry" or develops a community for singles, there is often the risk of inadvertently creating a pseudo dating or matchmaking service. While there is value in singles meeting other singles, the church also needs to provide an amply diverse community where single young adults can be integrated into the larger church community. Many singles become alienated when the church preaches "God's will for you is to be married" at them rather than celebrating their choice to be single or sharing their not unusual pain or loneliness.

Young adults not only are able to receive from the community, they can also give by serving the community in a variety of ways. The greatest untapped resources of creativity, wisdom, and openness for the church may be in its youth population. But the church must have the attitude that the young adults are needed and are valuable in order for young adults to feel needed and valuable. Wayne, an engineer, says: "I began teaching Sunday school for junior high young people when I was in college. I've been doing it for almost ten years, now, and I've probably learned more by teaching these young people than I would have if I spent ten years sitting in an adult Sunday school class. I feel that young adults can teach children and youth as well as adults. I hope that the church doesn't lose out on the creative energy of the young adult by not allowing us to serve the church."

The sharing that goes on in a church community is different from the sharing that goes on in secular social groups, for the church is challenged to struggle with issues dealing with the meaning of being a faithful people today. From the point of view of many young adults, however, the church shies away from the issues that are pertinent to them. Sexual ethics for singles, partnership models of marriage, discerning vocational calls are among the relevant issues for young adults; often the church is either unready or afraid to delve into them.

Vince, a seminary student, argues:"I believe that there is a biblical basis for an ethic of sexuality that relates to sexual ethics for singles that has integrity, that is Christian. But I know that most churches wouldn't touch the subject with a ten-foot pole. If we are serious about educational ministry with young adults—and if we want to be relevant in this world—then this is one topic the church must deal with."

Lisa and Keith, who have been married for two years, say:"We would like the church to provide a forum in which different styles of living out the partnership model of marriage can be explored. When we have attended conservative churches, they offered many courses for young married couples, but we were told in these classes that the man needs to have control over the relationship and have sole decision-making power. This argument was carefully backed by various Bible verses, and we were made to feel that we were seeking a life-style that was nonbiblical. In the mainline denomination churches, though, we were surprised because this issue isn't even dealt with. Are we the only two people in the mainline churches who are struggling with and exploring creative ways to live a life-style of partnership? We don't think so. At least we hope we're not. The question of whose career is more important, how we can both be involved in active parenting, and how we can live out our faith in terms of our investment of money and time are all very important to us."

Another issue that young adults face is the question of vocational call. Many are unclear about what to do with their lives in this fast-moving society. Providing guidance in choosing careers, in making ethical decisions about vocations, and in helping young adults to see their vocation as a call by God must be a feature of any church's educational ministry.

A caring, loving community that is dealing with relevant life-and-faith issues also needs to have enlivening experiences of celebration together. As in the story of the road to Emmaus where the two men recognize Jesus as the bread is being broken, so does a community recognize Christ as the bread is broken and its common life is celebrated. As in other aspects of community life, worship needs to be relevant and suited to that particular community. Young adults long for worship services where the style and the content of worship reflect who they are in this society, which speak to how they ought to be as faithful people in this society. Traditional styles of worship are important, but there are different ways of expressing the joy of life and the celebration of God without adhering strictly to formalized styles. New hymns can be sung, new dances can be danced, and new symbols encouraged as the faith of the young adult finds new avenues of expression in the '80s and '90s.

The young adult period of a person's life is frightening as well as exciting. The church can benefit from the creative energy of young adults as it enters into ministry for and with them.

9

Listening
to Other Voices

Edesio Sánchez-Cetina

We who have grown up in the Reformed tradition have learned that the Bible is the fundamental source for our Christian obedience. Our reflection on any area of theology and Christian experience—our thinking about all areas of human life—should be informed by biblical teachings. When we enter into the specifics of church education, we are dealing with a field where Christians think through some decisive questions: How are we to live faithfully in today's world? How are we to keep our integrity as human beings and join with others to reach the same goal?

In our educational practice, the Bible must remain central. So it is important to refocus our attention on the Bible and the way we interpret it. This essay will discuss the need to listen to "other voices" as we study the Bible. When studying the Bible, what voices do we usually hear? Whose voices do we allow to enter into dialogue with us as we open the Bible? What place do we give to these other voices, especially those we do not normally hear, or of whose existence we perhaps are not even aware?

What I want to do here is to call your attention to the crucial role of these other voices. Their contributions are decisive if we are to have a full understanding of the biblical message. Indeed, our understanding of the Bible remains radically incomplete when we do not allow other voices to interact with ours.

The importance of this interaction can be seen in various ways. *First*, we bring to our reading of the Bible all our reality as human beings. We belong to a particular social class, race, sex; we have our own cultural and moral heritages, our specific world views and ideologies. When we read the Bible, what emerges is greatly influenced by these perspectives. What we grasp is influenced by who we are. Our reading is a blend of two messages: the object of our knowledge and the perspective from which we acquire it.

Second, we live in a world that has put us all "under a single roof." International economic and political ties and the mass media have made everyone participants in world events. It is impossible to escape the influence and impact of things happening around us, both near and far. It is impossible to get away from participating, consciously or not, positively or not, in actions that influence the lives of others.

A recent immigrant to the United States was quoted in *Time* (October 15, 1984) as saying: "I am a German who has lived in the United States for only a few months. Pride in being a member of a nation is not bad. But I notice that this feeling blocks out everything outside the United States. Your nation is a beautiful and powerful one. Yet it is part of this world. Nearly everything that happens in other countries affects the United States, and vice versa. I think Americans should be more aware of this."

Third, we Christians have been called to a single mission: to help enable human life to be more human and to make this world a healthy home for all God's creation.

All three of these insights demand a twofold liberation, a liberation of the Bible and of ourselves. The messsage of the Bible needs to be freed of the chains we impose on it to keep it from saying things we prefer to remain hidden. We tend to let the Bible tell only what we want to be its message; we ask it to express our own views. And our own views need to be free from our various blindnesses, from the relativity of our perspectives, and from the restraints imposed by our own desires.

The voices of others can accomplish this liberation. Taking seriously the voices of others will open up blind spots and will correct our narrowness of mind. They will unlock perspectives previously hidden by all that has conditioned our seeing and hearing—our doctrinal biases, world views, ideologies, class interests, sex, race, life-style, and values.

These other voices belong to a complex spectrum of persons. Because of their closeness to us in class, race, or ideology, some belong to the same group to whom I am addressing these words: the white Christian community in the United States. But differences in sex or in age make them important partners in dialogue. Most Bible studies in the United States are oriented to adult males. The loud voices are normally those from the academic world—usually dominated by males—and filtered to us through male ministers or Bible study leaders. Seldom does the female perspective enter the exchange. Practically never do we hear the voices of youth and children. How revealing it would be to have children ask the questions in Bible study! How much difference it might make to use a book by a woman author, interpreting the Bible from a feminist perspective! When intergenerational and intergender Bible study is done, the way is clear for a more faithful interpretation. The whole Christian community then becomes the subject of interpretation; all members of it have the opportunity to share their voices.

However, because of their commitment to similar values, these kindred voices do not help the Christian community to free itself from the many blind spots and distorted views. Here it is that the voices of Christians who belong to other communities and social groups become essential. These believers are often experienced by the white community as being voiceless. Their powerless position makes it impossible for them to be heard by the

dominant class. Their books—if published—seldom reach
the desks of scholars and ministers of the white community. Some of these persons live in a neighborhood quite
close by, or in a ghetto, or on a reservation. Others are
farther away, in one of the poor countries in Asia, Africa,
or Latin America. We call them, for lack of a better term,
Third World Christians. "Third World" does not connote
geographical distinctions only, it also speaks about socioeconomic differences. Race, color, social class, cultural
and religious heritages, and history have made the majority of Third World Christians part of an unjust and
oppressive reality. They are usually the poor.

These are voices that the white Christian community
should not have the misfortune to avoid hearing. For North
Atlantic Christianity, hearing them is a matter of life and
death. The fate of North American Christianity depends,
to a great deal, on its openness to the influence of the
voices from the Third World.

The poor are important for Bible study for several reasons. The Bible grew out of the historical and socioeconomic context of the oppressed poor. It was written largely
to account for the way the God of the Bible entered human
history to free an oppressed people from slavery. The
exodus event is the core of the Old Testament; it plays no
less a role in the New Testament. The Bible speaks again
and again in laws and prophetic vision of a society where
the widow, the fatherless, and "the stranger" (a technical
phrase in the King James Version of the Old Testament
for the poor) can be authentic human beings. Frequently
the Bible startles its readers by presenting a God who asks
for a deliberate choice to stand with and for the poor. It
tells of a God who regularly makes unpopular choices:
electing to make a group of slaves God's people (Deut.
7:7), choosing to make the poor the locus of the divine
mission (Luke 4:18–19; Matt. 11:2–6), proclaiming that it
is the poor who are the owners of the kingdom of God
(Luke 6:20; Matt. 5:3).

If the Bible was written to tell the story of the God who chooses to be on the side of the poor, it must have been written largely from the perspective of the poor and oppressed. If this is so, then the perspective of the poor becomes essential to understand the biblical message. "The sociologically poor are important to the gospel," writes Orlando Costas, "not just because of their situation, but also because of their kerygmatic significance: They disclose the death of God's justice and the path that must be followed in order to be reconciled to God" (*The Integrity of Mission*; Harper & Row, 1979).

The poor are the privileged interpreters of the Bible because they can more easily recognize that they reexperience the biblical story. When they read the Bible they see its drama relived in their own lives—in their own hopes and sorrows, their sufferings and struggles. In their reading of the Bible, they quickly mix their own lives in with the Bible and the Bible in with their lives.

Here are two examples. The first is provided by Carlos Mesters in "The Use of the Bible in Christian Communities of the Common People":

> Once, in Goiás [Brazil], we read the passage in the New Testament (Acts 17:19) where an angel of the Lord came and freed the apostles from jail. The pastoral worker asked his people: "Who was the angel?" One of the women present gave this answer: "Oh, I know. When Bishop Dom Pedro Casaldáliga was attacked in his house and the police surrounded it with machine guns, no one could get in or out and no one knew what was going on exactly. So this little girl sneaked in without being seen, got a little message from Pedro, ran to the airport, and hitched a ride to Goiana where the bishops were meeting. They got the message, set up a big fuss, and Dom Pedro was set free. So that little girl was the angel of the Lord. And it's really the same sort of thing."(*The Challenge of Basic Christian Communities*, ed. by Sergio Torres and John Eagleson, p. 207; Orbis Books, 1981)

The other example is from *The Gospel in Solentiname*. The passage of the Bible being studied was Matthew 2:12–23, where Herod seeks to kill the infant Jesus. It was read on a Sunday, in the context of martial law in Nicaragua. That day, just before the Mass, a National Guard patrol had come to inspect the houses in Solentiname. The Bible was studied in an atmosphere of fear. Read what one of the women said:

> That's just like what goes on nowadays, and it's because any-one that is struggling for the liberation of the oppressed, he himself is a Christ, and then there's a Herod, and what we're seeing is the living story of the life of Jesus. And more Herods will come along, because whenever there's someone struggling for liberation there's someone who wants to kill him, and if they can kill him they will. How happy Somoza would have been if Ernesto and Fernando had died when they were little kids so they wouldn't be teaching all this. It's perfectly clear that the business of Herod and Christ, we have it right here. (Ernesto Cardenal, *The Gospel in Solentiname*, p. 72; Orbis Books, 1976)

The other voices, I maintain, are crucial because they function as a reminder—sometimes a painful one—of four realities. In the *first* place, the *hermeneutical subject* is more inclusive than exclusive. In biblical interpretation the powerless, those on the periphery—as subjects of interpretation—can have a more privileged position than those in controlling positions.

In the *second* place, the *content* of the biblical message may not always have the shape white Christian scholarship has given it. It is amazing, for instance, to see specialists in Matthew disagreeing about the structure of the Gospel. However, none of them seem to find central that which someone like Gustavo Gutiérrez finds:

> Let us consider Matthew's Gospel. Its first four chapters deal with the birth of Jesus and the preparation for his mission. Its last three chapters deal with his death resulting from that

mission and with the resurrection; through the resurrection the Father confirms the meaning of Jesus' task. The twenty-one chapters between these two sections give us the preaching of Jesus. They begin with the blessing of the poor (Matt. 5); they end with the assertion that we meet Christ himself when we go out to the poor with concrete acts (Matt. 25). So the teaching of Jesus is framed in a context that moves *from the poor to the poor*. This shows us that only in such a perspective can we comprehend the meaning of the Kingdom promised to the poor. (*The Challenge of Basic Christian Communities*, p. 121)

In the *third* place, these other voices are helpful because they point toward *the place where God wants to be found*. The exodus story gives us a hermeneutical axis to help us interpret God's salvific action in history. Both Exodus 3:7–14 and Exodus 6:2–8, by structure and content, tell that the revelation of God's mighty name and communication of God's being are done in the context of the cry for liberation from injustice and oppression. What occasions the revelation of God's unique name is the suffering of an oppressed people. Today, in order to see where God is acting, it is essential for us to be in solidarity with the oppressed poor. Their voices and cries help those who have known only economic privilege to rid themselves of the siren voices of gods and wicked powers that interfere with the reading and hearing of the Bible. These other voices help the reader of the Bible hear God's true voice. This in turn will be a help in discovering and unmasking the false gods who often control biblical interpretation. The voices of the poor thus become an emancipating force.

In the *fourth* place, the voices of the Third World poor will become a tool to *the way* to grasp the message of the Bible in its fullness. They help liberate interpreters from academic oppression. They give the exegetical efforts an often missing balance. As Carlos Mesters says, "Biblical exegetes, using their heads and their studies, can come fairly close to Abraham; but their feet are a long way from

Abraham. The common people are very close to Abraham with their feet."

The voices of the poor not only free the interpreter from academia, they also offer help in approaching the Bible in a more integral and holistic way. There is no tearing away from the Scriptures of abstract concepts such as peace, hunger, love, and salvation, as is so common in North Atlantic biblical studies. For the poor, the Bible speaks of human beings, of people whose lives are saved or threatened in concrete historical situations. In those situations all these concepts are interwoven, and only so can they be properly interpreted.

The voices of the poor, of children and women, are also important to help in the discovery of texts and concepts that are central in the Bible and of crucial importance for today's church. If we listen to them, texts and concepts that have been kept silent by ideological reasons will begin to speak out loudly.

The reading of the Bible is a social endeavor. Therefore, other voices should be welcomed for interaction and also for their influence on our interpretation and understanding. The hearing of these can reenact something of what the Pentecostal community experienced in Acts 2, where social inclusiveness was both a reality and a part of Joel's vision of God's benediction:

> And in the last days it shall be, God declares,
> that I will pour out my Spirit upon all flesh,
> and your sons and your daughters shall prophesy,
> and your young men shall see visions,
> and your old men shall dream dreams;
> yea, and on my menservants and my maidservants in those
>   days
> I will pour out my Spirit; and they shall prophesy.
>   (Acts 2:17–18; see Joel 2:28–29)

10

Adult Education:
A Recent Phenomenon

Jocelyn Hill

Looking around the corner of the '80s and beginning the march toward the twenty-first century, church educators envision a sea of adults. The baby boomers are in their forties; the over sixty-fives are almost one half of the population: and today's teenagers, who sometimes question whether they will ever *live* to grow up, may be listed on the church rolls as young adults. In what ways are we preparing for this population bulge? Where are we headed in adult education? Will the classroom setting become obsolete? Given the slower rate of change in adult programming, when will the computer reach adult learners in the church? Will mainline Protestants such as the Presbyterians continue to put a priority on intentional education?

Where Have We Been?

Adult church education as we know it has a relatively short history. Knowing this history is integral to knowing what we are now doing; it explains the myriad of programs, curricula, methods, classes, schools, and retreats that go under the current umbrella of adult education.

Our story begins in the '40s. Traveling down the road of the *Uniform Lessons Series* and single-sex classes, adult education began to expand. Groups for single young adults appeared, meeting the demand of programs for service-men and working women. The postwar back-to-church period of the '50s saw the beginning of the couples classes, built around shared experiences of the war and the baby explosion.

In *Heads of Heaven, Feet of Clay* (Pilgrim Press, 1983) Charles McCollough documents the history of the past four decades. He reminds us of the various movements that have influenced adult education in mainline Protestantism. With an emphasis on academic theology in more progressive churches in the '50s, some Presbyterian adults began to tackle the heady theology of men like Barth, Brunner, the Niebuhrs, and Tillich. Fanning this flickering flame of adult education was the *Christian Faith and Life* curriculum, a major contribution of the Presbyterian Church in the U.S.A. In some congregations adult education became "small-group education," as the group dynamics movement hit the church, followed by the human potential movement.

The *Covenant Life Curriculum* was launched in the '60s by the Presbyterian Church in the U.S., with its primary emphasis on adults. The political and social turbulence of the '60s forced the church to test out in adult seminars the secular theologies of Harvey Cox and Dietrich Bonhoeffer, the Black theology of Eldridge Cleaver and Martin Luther King, the shocking statement of Bishop John A. T. Robinson in *Honest to God*. Short-term studies focusing on issues were a natural addition to the curriculum for adults, occasionally culminating in education for social action. Encounter groups took place on weekend retreats.

The '70s led some adults into curriculum building, a self-directed learning approach, complete with needs assessment and the designing of programs to meet those findings. "Who am I?" was the existential question of the period, as adult classes clarified values, did rating scales, and answered questionnaires. In 1978, *Christian Education: Shared Approaches*, the first major effort in interdenominational curriculum since the beginning of the *International Lessons*, offered adults four different approaches to biblical and ethical studies.

In that same decade, the voice of the Third World began to be heard through liberation theology. Terms like "inclusiveness" and "racial-ethnic" began to impact adult education. Consciousness-raising about singles, women, racial-ethnic minorities, the aging, and the handicapped found its way into special studies, which were a part of denominational thematic emphases.

Also in the '70s the "ages and stages" theory of learning — highlighted for adults by Erik Erikson and Daniel Levinson and made popular in Gail Sheehy's *Passages*—encouraged the study of such personal and existential concerns as parenting, life after divorce, and mid-life crises. James Fowler's application of the stages theory to faith development began a process among adults that surfaced in many adult courses on "the faith journey"—the sharing of one's own pilgrimage.

In the '80s educators like Parker Palmer and theologians like Henri Nouwen and Thomas Merton have encouraged many adults to a deepening of the spiritual life. Charles McCollough describes an educational process that he names "other-directed faith education," whose goal is defined as "faith in the divine mystery of personal growth towards God."

During the decades just highlighted, many adult Protestants—perhaps the majority—continued traditional education in their congregations, unaware of the movements, leaders, or theologians just named. Regional and national educational staffs and committees have provided resources and leader training, sometimes initiating and sometimes following the trends emerging in church and society. At whatever level or stage at which persons may have joined the process, the interest, involvement, and expansion of adult education has been a phenomenon in the recent life of the church.

What's Happening Now?

At this point in our history, what are Protestant adults doing? Here are some representative samples. Sixty or seventy members of one church gather for an annual retreat in a setting by the sea. One participant says, "The adult retreat is the event I look forward to most during the year. I have time to think and talk about things that matter, apart from my responsibilities at home and in my job. The program is always varied and stimulating, and I get a chance to be with a group of adults completely unlike my own circle of friends." In one small-group session, a twenty-five-year-old single woman is involved in a discussion with a middle-aged man, two persons over sixty-five, and a thirty-five-year-old executive who was recently separated from his wife. They are brainstorming ways that the community of faith can be a sign of God's grace in the world today, following an address on the topic by a qualified resource leader. Opportunities for other configurations of diverse ages and backgrounds are given through the sharing of meals, recreation, and worship.

Members of a small discussion class, who had met together for a number of years, decided they had talked and studied issues for too long. What had they accomplished? They had explored biblical backgrounds, discussed complexities of some major concern, dealt with decision-making. They were better informed as individuals, but for what? So they targeted one issue of concern to the majority of the group—public education. Coupled with study, they did interviews, made on-site visits, and attended meetings of the school board. Finally, they were convinced that some concrete action should be taken. They organized a committee on quality education in the community and sought to elect three new members to the school board who were committed to changes that the group felt needed to be made. When this essay was being written, they were working hard to elect those persons—no longer acting in the name of their class or church. This group discovered ways to put their concern into action; that is, to "do the word."

On Thursday evenings, a group of adults from two congregations—one suburban, one inner city—is engaged in a peacemaking study. The course was designed and is being carried out by leadership from both churches. Part of an enrollment fee goes to supply each participant with a packet of study materials; all participants are given specific assignments, to which they commit time and effort for the duration of their ten-week study. At this point in their course, no one is sure what the outcome will be. Group action? Individual peacemaking efforts? An agreement to study together as a support group for sharing and further study of perhaps another issue?

One congregation that is racially plural and has persons from several ethnic backgrounds has seen a need for some kind of core curriculum: Bible, Presbyterian heritage, personal growth concerns, ethical studies relating to current issues, and cultural appreciation. Leaders are designing a curriculum for a three-year period. All adults will be encouraged to participate in a balanced program of study, electing courses from each area of emphasis during the three years. Courses will be offered during the church school hour, in weeknight programs, in retreats, and in a special school. The curriculum ranges from the *Cooperative Uniform Series* to a study of Mexican-American heritage.

Where Do We Go?

In the light of our history, from the vista of the mid-'80s, how do we view the next decade in adult education? For what do we need to be planning?

First of all, this decade devoted to peacemaking calls us to plan for adult education with a global perspective. In curriculum development we must continue partnership across denominations and seek partnerships with fellow Christians around the world. When possible, multilingual materials, written by Third World as well as Western partners, should appear in our week-by-week curriculum— not just as special studies produced by councils of churches or international mission divisions. Church education for adults—not just headlines and high technology—should reflect our shrinking planet.

Global education must be intentionally lived out. Just as some presbyteries and conferences now offer a global village week or weekend with a sharing of study and fellowship and cultural heritage, so must our congregations become global villages themselves. Persons from other cultures and countries should increasingly be part of our educational settings—sometimes deliberately invited, sometimes just warmly welcomed. Congregations that are not located near an international community may join together in sponsoring visits from Christians in other nations; they may also work to fund visits to other countries.

Second, in a move that is not hostile to the global perspective, we Presbyterians must seek to retain our Reformed heritage. No matter what the world crises, national and cultural trends, theologies, or learning styles, we must continue to give opportunity for every generation to learn and appropriate what it means to be a Presbyterian. Whether education employs books, video cassettes, or computers, Presbyterians must become acquainted with a living heritage of their faith in such a way that they can make a mature response on their own. Adults who have passed through a confirmation class at some earlier stage of their lives need to stop again at the door of John Calvin. They need a speaking acquaintance with the confessional statements, old and new; they need to struggle with what it means to confess their faith in their own marketplaces and condominium complexes.

Settings for study may increasingly require flex time and place, but the church's educational ministry must give a priority *to* and demand a priority *of* commitment to the exploration of the faith. The very nature of the Reformed faith calls us to keep "re-forming"—reshaping who we are, not in the light of our own image but in the light of what God has called this particular church to be, through the centuries and as this century turns a page. While rejoicing in our diversity, we need to hold on to our particularity. "Who am I?" was never a bad question; we just failed to make it plural. Adult education has a mandate to reclaim and restate who we are as a Presbyterian family.

Third, in the midst of the increasing availability and use of computers and whatever inventions of high tech await us, adult education for the next decade must structure opportunities for valuing the personal. Classroom settings and learning styles must demonstrate and give opportunity for relationship. Recent studies of those who live in a person-to-machine world show that it is difficult to reenter the world of person to person. All that we have learned about group process may have to be accompanied by basic communication skills. In a time when more of us may elect to shop and bank and work at home, the church may be one of the few settings where people will seek community. The traditional church school class, whose members have stayed together and learned to care for one another through the years, may be a model that we need to recapture in short-term groupings. Although our curriculum be global in perspective and Presbyterian in content, we must still invite persons to be at home with one another in the presence of a living and loving God.

Parker Palmer, in his book *To Know as We Are Known: A Spirituality of Education*, p. 83 (Harper & Row, 1983), suggests that "teachers must also create emotional space in the classroom, space that allows feelings to arise and be dealt with." Adults of the '90s may need to return to some of the "getting-in-touch-with-our feelings" of the '70s. This time around, adult planners need to structure "high touch" clearly in the context of the family of God's people, called not to therapy groups but to discipleship and responsible living with one another.

Fourth, however we envision Christians in the twenty-first century, it seems a certainty that they will be searching for a center for their lives. Whether we call it a "spirituality of education" or "contemplative education," we are talking about education in the spiritual disciplines.

Henri Nouwen, in *Making All Things New* (Harper & Row, 1981), reminds us that a spiritual life requires effort and discipline. Parker Palmer (p. 69) invites us to structure that discipline in the classroom setting, with occasional directed silence, listening, creating "a space in which obedience to truth is practiced." Can Presbyterians, who usually express community with God and with each other in words, also discover the wonder of community in silence? Can the baby boomers and youth of the '80s, who work with computers and jog with headsets on, discover meaning in contemplation? The works of Thomas Kelly, Thomas Merton, and Henri Nouwen are already finding their way into our curriculum. I suggest that adult education of the future will need more and more to include the dimension of "other-directed faith education," both in content and in process.

But learning to listen to the inner spirit of God must always be in tandem with the written Word of God. The Reformed tradition insists on the primacy of Scripture. In recent decades we have excelled in talking about the Bible but often have failed to provide opportunity for persons to hear and respond to that Word themselves.

What issues will shape the cutting edge of the '90s? Whatever has been projected by *Megatrends* will be passé, but Presbyterian adults will continue to be concerned and involved. The inability of strategies for social education to sweep the whole church in no way proves that it is futile to prepare adults to work for change in society. Adult programming must be increasingly *intentional* in education for mission. Too often adults have been engaged in giving an issue the once-over-lightly in classes that are considered avant-garde because they have talked openly about abortion or homophobia. It is easy to listen to an expert give us the facts, followed by lively discussions, and then to feel that we have dealt with an issue. We conclude a mini-course on economic justice without its reordering our priorities or life-styles or calling us to action. The fragility of life on this planet demands the creative action of Christians around the world who not only talk about issues but roll up their sleeves and become involved for the sake of our Creator God.

John Fry, back in the '60s, first called for learning in "contract groups" in his book *A Hard Look at Adult Christian Education* (Westminster Press, 1961). Small churches and large, rural and urban, must bid for the time and commitment of some adults to address the issues in depth. Adult planners must provide the practical resources, encouragement, and support to enable those groups to act.

As I visualize adult education with its need to be global, Presbyterian, and intentional in providing for relationship, spiritual discipline, and action, I see a need for multi-faceted groupings and settings. With a large segment of the church population in middle age or over sixty-five, adults need more opportunity to cross peer lines. Retreats of whatever duration can be held in back yards, in another congregation's parlor, on college campuses, or in spacious offices, if centers are not readily accessible or affordable. Smaller congregations can be yoked with one another for programming and for sharing of resources and leadership. Church education of the future may necessarily be ecumenical. We could begin by initiating special studies and conferences with neighboring congregations. Children and youth seem to have a monopoly on field trips and work camps; adults who get beyond the parameters of their own communities also have visions of the human community that can come in the sharing of ideas and work in another culture. Churches could encourage and sponsor the learning of other languages as we explore other cultural histories and life-styles.

The arts must find a central place in our methodology with adults. "Right brain" learning will be needed to kindle the imagination of machine-oriented computerists. Adult educators must work harder to tap the media for education. Video recorders increasingly grace our homes. The development of more lively video cassettes and the creative marketing of materials provide a continuing challenge to reach learners in whatever settings they already find themselves.

Adult leaders and teachers are flocking to workshops and training sessions provided by our denomination. As we move into another decade, we have a corner on the adult education market. We must meet that opportunity with creative energy—reminding ourselves, however, that the kingdom will not come in more programs and resources. Under the Spirit of God, our challenge will be to invite adults to join us in discovering the meaning of discipleship in the age in which we live.

11

Social Education for Exiled People

Dieter T. Hessel

Exile, even more than exodus, is a theological key to educational ministry in North America at the close of this century. Exodus remains the most pertinent biblical paradigm for oppressed communities in overtly dominated societies such as those in South Africa, El Salvador, Afghanistan, or the Philippines. But exile is an instructive paradigm for us who suddenly find ourselves living in a strange place with power dissipated, dreams soured, and Babylonians in charge. Here we feel personally disappointed about unmet social expectations. We mainline Protestants also recognize that our moral power has dissipated and the Telechurch of New Right Religion now infects public attitudes. Meanwhile our federal government has failed to meet basic human needs even as it continues to implement deadly plans of survival/salvation attuned to the imagery of Armaggedon. How shall we sing the Lord's song in this strange land? How do we express covenant faithfulness?

Our Situation

For a while we thought that American society, being "progressive," had agreed to seek racial justice, to avoid

Third World military intervention, and to meet basic human needs at home and abroad. But the consensus was shattered during the first half of the 1980s. Current national policy as publicly stated may not be overtly racist, militarist, or classist, but it is at least covertly so, and our deepening social crisis features violence and division. The social situation that we experience, in its pathology and promise, can be summarized as follows:

Most obvious is an obsession with national security that escalates the arms race while militarizing foreign relations. A growing number of Christians with ecumenical consciousness seek to counteract militarism through the movement for peacemaking. Equally ominous is the continued exploitation of Third and Fourth World peoples and the resources of their lands by local elites and military forces in collusion with large corporations and with our military assistance. In a critical, hopeful response, the church supports programs of hunger action and self-development, while undertaking acts of solidarity and sanctuary.

Meanwhile, in the United States there is a marked increase of racially motivated violence, as well as resurgent sexism, while affirmative action for minorities and women is officially disregarded. The church, though startled by such a rapid reversal of public commitment, continues to emphasize that institutionalized racism and sexism require structural solutions such as affirmative action and economic pressure (boycotts and divestment), along with education to overcome prejudice, and that the church should model these changes. At the same time, economic dislocation and a widening gap between rich and poor have displaced rapid economic growth as a fixture of American life. Though some groups in our society and church enjoy unprecedented prosperity, the proportion of poor people grows, and the policies of government deliberately ignore their plight or deny their claims to justice. Many middle-income households also experience unemployment and underemployment; they struggle grimly to survive in communities without adequate jobs or human services. In response, the church continues to enlist new leadership and the resources of its members in the struggle for economic justice and in ministries of community action.

All this occurs in an ethos of ideological defense of the American way of life. Politicians and preachers join business leaders and pundits in reasserting that old-time religion of individual liberty, political Darwinism, and paternalistic charity. Having wrapped itself in flag and faith, such "fundamentalism" resists gender and racial equality, justice to the poor and powerless, reconciliation with enemies, and cultural pluralism. Nevertheless, many Christians, including Presbyterians, welcome and work for a multicultural, international household (the *oikos* in Ephesians) of women and men who care especially for vulnerable people and seek abundant community. Such a reconciling community works to overcome forces that would "exclude, dominate, or patronize others" and it pursues "fresh and responsible relations across every line of conflict, even at risk to national security" (Presbyterian Confession of 1967).

The preceding social analysis *cannot* be derived from the daily news alone. It reflects an exposure to the experience and viewpoint of the powerless, and it points to promising acts of Christian witness and ministry amid deepening social pathology. It is an expression of exilic theological consciousness in our time and place. Here under Babylonian siege, takeover, and dispersion, we too must learn how to experience the judgment of God on our covenant-breaking, religious-social system and consumptive way of life, while grasping the vision and life-style of hopeful sojourners who would become a faithful remnant. Knowing that we have broken covenant, we also need to follow Habakkuk's advice to the early exiles:

Write the vision;
   make it plain upon tablets,
   so they may run who read it.
For still the vision awaits its time;
   it hastens to the end—it will not lie.
If it seem slow, wait for it;
  . . . .
   the righteous shall live by faithfulness.
   (Habakkuk 2:2–4)

Dynamic Similarities

Our situation and responsibility as Christians in America are dynamically analogous in several ways to that of the Old Testament community of faith in exile. But although our situation is analogous, it is not parallel, since ours is a more complex society with new difficulties and opportunities. Our horizon of peril and promise is open and uncertain; our human action will not merely recapitulate theirs. Moreover, we are not as devastated by a "conquering force"; we are more in danger of being co-opted. Yet we have a dynamically analogous experience to sort out.

1. *We are confronted by oppressive or constricting realities—societal and psychic—that contradict what the biblical covenant ethic requires.* The current realities are summarized in the paragraphs above which describe our situation. But even that description of reality is understated in comparison with the language of the prophets and overstated in the eyes of many prosperous and relatively powerful Presbyterians.

Prophetic consciousness specializes in pungent, picturesque language to convey the judgment of God on the faithlessness of people, princes, and priests. Jeremiah 2: 20ff. compares faithless Judah to a stubborn ox, a wild vine, an insatiable prostitute, an ass in heat, a thief caught in wrongdoing. Jeremiah's temple sermon enjoins the people to live repentantly:

> For if you truly amend your ways and your doings, if you truly execute justice one with another, if you do not oppress the alien, the fatherless or the widow, or shed innocent blood in this place, and if you do not go after other gods to your own hurt, then I [the Sovereign God] will let you dwell in this place, in the land that I gave of old to your fathers for ever.
> (Jeremiah 7:5–7)

Much of the prophet's message is counterpoint to that covenant promise. His is a graphic portrayal of Yahweh, fed up with Judah's disobedience, and a resolute response to the Babylonian takeover of choice property and deportation of leaders. Exilic consciousness highlights the contradictions between the shalom vision and the covenant ethic, on one hand, and the people's idolatry, self-righteousness, and injustice, on the other.

Many social leaders and members of the community of faith did not see the contradictions then, nor do such leaders see those contradictions now. The prophetic message has always been received merely as bad news by those who benefit much from existing socioeconomic arrangements and who need to be optimistic about keeping ominous problems at bay or finding some new—if temporary—fix, be it technological or political. Prosperous Presbyterians and other mainline Christians today can become very impatient or offended by sharp criticism of national life or public advocacy of justice to the powerless on the part of the church. They and we together must learn how to admit our own complicity in the faithlessness of the American way of life.

2. *Our church and society also experience the clash between true and false prophets.* Often our privileged location in society and world keeps us out of touch with the poor or powerless and disposes us to welcome those who heal "the wound of [God's] people lightly, saying 'peace, peace,'

when there is no peace" (Jer. 6:14). The false prophet Hananiah assured the leaders of the people, "Thus says the LORD of hosts, the God of Israel: I have broken the yoke of the king of Babylon. Within two years, I will bring back to this place all the vessels . . . and all the exiles" (Jer. 28:2–3).

To make the point he broke the symbolic yoke that Jeremiah wore. Jeremiah responded by first saying, "Amen! May the LORD do so, . . . [Yet we should expect] war, famine, and pestilence. . . . As for the prophet who prophesies peace, when the word of that prophet comes to pass, then it will be known that the LORD has truly sent the prophet. . . . Listen, Hananiah, the LORD has not sent you, and you have made this people trust in a lie" (Jer. 28:6–9, 15).

We are going through an analogous experience of false prophesy regarding the health of American society and the prospects of peace with justice. Large segments of society and church do not recognize this because of ideological myopia and theological misperception, reinforced by an alienating insulation from the powerless and from ethnic/cultural pluralism.

Today's clash of true and false prophets occurs in secular political discourse, and it occurs in two ways throughout the church: *within* our Presbyterian congregations and governing bodies and *between* the ecumenical denominations and the New Right organizations. We must deal with this clash explicitly in our educational ministry. To do so requires that we explore the story of the exile in all its contemporary relevance, highlighting the dynamic connections between "then" and "now." Thus we develop fresh exilic theological consciousness in the community of faith. Such theological consciousness has definite ethical content which orients social praxis as well as prayer life.

Each congregation and group of Christians needs to teach the concrete personal and political meaning of such *qualities of faithfulness* as hope in God's future, justice for oppressed people, love for near and distant neighbors, preservation of basic human rights, care for the whole creation, responsible stewardship of power, and creative actions for peace across every line of hostility. Some implications are that the church shall express solidarity with victims of oppression and join in ministry with the poor, work for constructive changes of public policy in the direction of justice and peace, protest against dangerous or wicked enterprises that cloak their deeds in the name of freedom and security, stand with those whose moral witness involves civil disobedience, and warn against patterns of tribalism and anarchy in crucial areas of societal and international relations.

The struggle for faithfulness is not only within the church and in each of us. It is also between ecumenical denominations, such as the Presbyterian Church (U.S.A.), and New Right organizations and commentators who ridicule our witness to judgment and hope as either subversive of the American way of life or unrealistic for these times. In each community and church there are false prophets who would have American Christians trust in lies about the state of society, the mission of the church, and the future toward which God is moving the world. It is essential for us to clarify and communicate just what we ecumenical Protestants stand for in society today, given our struggle with the false prophets.

Recognizing our need to teach all members such a social ethic, consistent with the best of biblical-theological tradition and informed by historical experience, we developed a hundred-page overview, "Social Teaching of the Presbyterian Church," published as a special issue of *Church and Society* magazine, November/December 1984. It illumines the consistent and contextual patterns of social concern and articulates basic principles of Christian social ethics that are prominent in Presbyterian General Assembly statements from both northern and southern streams.

Just to review the basic social teachings of mainline

Protestantism is to feel ethically exiled; that is, to realize how much our society has abandoned the most elementary practices of covenant ethics. This is an especially ironic outcome for Presbyterians, who have social power and affirm a mandate "to work for the transformation of society,"counteracting a pernicious "human tendency to idolatry and tyranny" (Form of Government, 2.05). How can we make more of a difference in shaping a humane public ethic and just public policies in these times of wrenching change?

3. *Our exile is also a time for historical reinterpretation to comprehend God's judgment.* The original exile produced two theologically informed interpretations—Deuteronomic and Priestly—of the national history. Both of those interpretations highlight the covenant ethic and Israel's disobedience and at least begin to portray an alternate future. It would be a mistake to transpose their historically conditioned explanation of divine judgment to our quite different setting. But the community of faith today also has a shared responsibility to interpret in theological-ethical terms what has gone wrong and to begin thinking about the alternate future into which history, under God's judgment and grace, is moving. We should do this without expecting any quick fix to a cultural-economic-political crisis that has developed over time and will not soon progress toward justice and peace.

In the short run, we face a startling combination of seemingly intractable social ills. How shall we interpret this "time of troubles"? I borrow the phrase from Arnold Toynbee, keeping in mind his insight that times of troubles may lead either to collapse or to new creativity. In a time of troubles, problems mount much faster than do the hints of their resolution. It is also a time when the culture's virtues become its vices.

Along this line, a pressing new reality of our time is that rapid economic growth is no longer sustainable, as it was in that unrepeatable era of affluence after World War II. It cannot be sustained because of definite ecological limits and the wrong kind of production. Our society has forgotten that economics entails stewardship (*oikonomia*), with the purpose of providing sufficient sustenance for all. As William E. Gibson has observed:

> Stewardship in economics means making arrangements, constructing and maintaining a system, under which each person according to his or her gifts of talent and ability participates in the work of meeting the needs and enriching the life of the household. Each member contributes to the common enterprise; each has or receives enough for health and fulfillment. But since the household functions after the Fall, the social arrangements have to be such as to restrain the power, pride, and greed of any who would appropriate more than their fair share of the goods available, or who think they are the absolute owners of the materials they control so that they can do whatever they please without concern for the other members and without accountability to God. (From "The Challenge to Be Stewards," unpublished paper, 1984)

Instead of practicing stewardship, our society fosters production of ever more surplus goods and spectacular technologies for the sake of bigger profits, rather than for social service. Contemporary economic growth generates ever more poverty and *under*development in poor sectors and peripheral countries even as it *over*develops affluent sectors of powerful nations. Unwarranted religious faith in progress through increased production, mixed with a determination to master nature and society to satisfy selfish human desires, fuel modern society's over/underdevelopment. Democratic capitalism and collective socialism seem to agree in principle, though not in methods, on this agenda.

Our society follows this destructive path to "liberty and progress" by means that ignore basic rights to sustenance, widen the gap between rich and poor, and create a national security apparatus that will actually constrict life for more and more people. Dominant political forces in the 1980s still do not see this pattern to be oppressive and will continue to foster it in the short run, even though it contradicts biblical wisdom and the teachings of the Messiah whose name we invoke.

To perceive ourselves in such a collective cultural box is to become aware of our own developing exile situation and to generate passionate hope for new covenant. In a world of grim choices or "forced options," where wrenching changes are guaranteed, we can expect to experience collectively the judgment of God as never before.

Jeremiah told his generation of exiles that they would not live to see a resolution of troubles and a blessed return, so they should build for the future and "seek the welfare of the city where [God has] sent you" (Jer. 29:7). Let us hope that our exile will not last as long as seventy years, though it is quite apparent that it will continue into the next century with uncertain results.

Perhaps our church is no better prepared than was ancient Judah to deal with exilic reality, but it is equally as urgent for us to discern what the world is coming to and our path of faithfulness therein. Langdon Gilkey recently noted that the ethical (i.e., covenant consciousness) again comes center stage when culture shows itself to be ambiguous and we realize how destructive as well as creative can be the uses of science, technology, industrialism, and even democracy. "Now the creative results of action are not so much dependent on the accumulation of knowledge, instruments or institutions as on the character of the human users thereof, and so on *how* they decide to use them" ("Theology of Culture and Christian Ethics," *The Annual of the Society of Christian Ethics*, 1984).

4. *Exile dispersion revitalizes mission.* In the biblical exile, the people of God were scattered throughout the Middle Eastern world, there to discover a servant mission. Dispersion has been recapitulated in the twentieth century

as the global missionary movement culminates in the ecumenical church. The church now crosses ethnic and national lines throughout the whole inhabited world—the
oikumene—and it looks forward to worldwide community
that is pluralistic in culture and politically just. The ecumenically mature church also undertakes mutuality, or
partnership, in mission that cares for the fate of the earth
and its people. Now we are receiving the ministry of the
younger, Third World churches to us. They are present
with us to help us hear the gospel multiculturally. They
prod us to become truly cosmopolitan.

In diaspora, the people of God were liberated, against
their will, from the Jerusalem temple cult. They were liberated for corporate messianic service: to share covenant
faith with the nations and to help establish justice throughout the earth. (See Isa. 42:1–4.) No doubt the Israelites
of the sixth century B.C.E. were also enlightened by their
relocation in such great cities as Babylon, an impressive
technological, artistic, and trade center, where they did
the creative theological writing that resulted in the Hebrew
Bible.

The prime task of exile theology in any profoundly trou-
bled era is to discern and express what new thing God is
doing in response to covenant broken and remnant dis-
persed. Exilic theology envisions a new covenant written
upon the heart and a future when the people will "know
the LORD" (Jer. 31:31–34; cf. Hosea 4).

Just as the Gospels incorporate the exilic theme of a
servant messianic community, so the late New Testament
letters of Hebrews and 1 Peter utilize explicit exile language. The famous roll call of pioneers in faith declares
them (and us) to be "strangers and exiles on the earth,"
people who "desire a better country" and for whom God
prepares New Jerusalem (Heb. 11:13–16). Ecumenical
Christians think not in terms of lasting cities here but
understand themselves to be, throughout exile time, "a
chosen race, a royal priesthood, a holy nation, God's own

people" witnessing to the light of Christ (1 Peter 2:9). Such a witness by ecumenical Christians requires that their ecclesiastical and social decisions be ethically mature.

5. *Faithfulness is renewed in covenant community among sojourning people.* Covenant praxis will be renewed in a nurturing community that develops a whole life together of revitalized liturgy, teaching, and witness.

Exile is a time for concentrated attention to the lively heritage of biblical story and church history. It is a time to bring that tradition to bear in worship, nurture, and mission engagement focused on justice and peace. For us that covenanting may be facilitated by keying our life together around the confessions of the church as well as theological emphases of the liturgical year and common lectionary. Exile is not a time for turning inward; it is time for articulate, vigorous witness to counteract fatalism and its twin, cynicism, in a strange land that has domesticated Christian faith to serve destructive living.

Leaders in Reformed educational ministry, instead of proceeding "as usual," need to think in terms of learning an alternate way of living by participating in a covenant community—a community of faith that demands a discipline of its members and teaches faithfulness by what it does. All available talent and methodological creativity should be brought to bear to help the church discern and demonstrate what God is doing in the world and with us in exile. Specifically:

• We need to give more direct educational attention to relearning the biblical story and to informed use of the story in "faith-full" liturgical language and symbols. In corporate worship, prayer retreats, and household rituals, our prayers must grapple with God's judgment.

• We need to explore social reality in more depth and teach a coherent social ethic that is expressive of our common pilgrimage in these times.

• We need to learn how to listen to Christians from Third World churches on every continent, as these Christians call us to faithfulness through confessional integrity and new steps of justice and peace.

• We need to link liturgies of the Word, liberating Bible study, and serious education in social analysis and ethics with concrete acts of ministry as bold servant people.

In the biblical exile, the congregation itself came into being as a social form. How shall the church reform in its parish expression to be socially responsible to covenant today? With whom shall we work to seek the welfare of the city where we find ourselves? We are called to witness to Messiah Jesus, the New Covenanter with whom we die and rise. We are obligated to be vigorously connected with the ecumenical mission of the larger church. Such covenanting and connecting forms of the church may be built up by base communities that are small enough to nurture each other and do ministry together. Whatever the variations, active communities of faith exist for the sake of the New Human Community that God is creating.

Welcome to educational ministry in this exile time!

Contributors

EDWARD A. DOWEY is Archibald Alexander Professor of the History of Christian Doctrine, Princeton Theological Seminary.

MARY DUCKERT is Associate for Children's Resources and Program, the Program Agency of the Presbyterian Church (U.S.A.).

FREDA A. GARDNER is Associate Professor of Christian Education, Princeton Theological Seminary.

DIETER T. HESSEL is Associate for Social Education, the Program Agency of the Presbyterian Church (U.S.A.).

JOCELYN HILL is Associate for Christian Education of the Mecklenburg Presbytery, Presbyterian Church (U.S.A.).

JAMES C. HUFFSTUTLER is Pastor of the First United Presbyterian Church, San Bernardino, California.

MARY PAIK is a student at San Francisco Theological Seminary.

EDESIO SÁNCHEZ-CETINA is a minister of the Presbyterian Church in Mexico.

JACK L. STOTTS is President of Austin Theological Seminary.

BARBARA A. WITHERS is Associate for Youth Education, the Program Agency of the Presbyterian Church (U.S.A.).

D. CAMPBELL WYCKOFF is Thomas W. Synnott Professor of Christian Education, Emeritus, Princeton Theological Seminary.